THE MAGNA CARTA PLAYS

THE MAGNA CARTA PLAYS

RANSOMED
by Howard Brenton

KINGMAKERS
by Anders Lustgarten

WE SELL RIGHT
by Timberlake Wertenbaker

PINK GIN
by Sally Woodcock

OBERON BOOKS
LONDON

This collection first published in 2015 by Oberon Books Ltd
521 Caledonian Road, London N7 9RH
Tel: +44 (0) 20 7607 3637 / Fax: +44 (0) 20 7607 3629
e-mail: info@oberonbooks.com
www.oberonbooks.com

A catalogue record for this book is available from the British Library.

PB ISBN: 9781783192939
E ISBN: 9781783192946

Cover image by Feast Creative

Converted
by CPI Group (UK) Ltd, Croydon, CR0 4YY.

The Magna Carta Plays
A Salisbury Playhouse Production

RANSOMED
by Howard Brenton

Yury Stanovich Koba	**Tim Frances**
Caroline Montfichet	**Juliet Howland**
Mrs Maddeley Coach	**Frances Jeater**
Roger Sylvester	**Mark Meadows**
Canon Simon St John	**Michael Mears**
Police Constable Harold Budd	**Ben Stott**
Detective Inspector Ellie Baxter	**Joanna Van Kampen**

KINGMAKERS
by Anders Lustgarten

Earl Grabber	**Tim Frances**
Duke Venal	**Trevor Michael Georges**
Lady Plunder	**Juliet Howland**
Sprocket	**Mark Meadows**
Lord Lamprey	**Michael Mears**
King Henry III	**Ben Stott**

WE SELL RIGHT
by Timberlake Wertenbaker

Older Woman	**Frances Jeater**
Older Woman	**Vivienne Rochester**
Girl	**Joanna Van Kampen**

PINK GIN
by Sally Woodcock

Jasper	**Tim Frances**
President	**Trevor Michael Georges**
Angelica	**Vivienne Rochester**

Other roles played by members of the company

THE CREATIVE TEAM

The Creative Team

Director	**Gareth Machin**
Designer	**Ellan Parry**
Lighting Designer	**Johanna Town**
Sound Designer & Composer	**Helen Skiera**
Movement Director	**Asha Jennings-Grant**
Video Designer	**Mark Noble**
Fight Director	**Paul Benzing**
Voice & Dialect Coach	**Kay Welch**
Assistant Director	**Jo Newman**
Casting Assistant	**Kirsty Airlie**

The Production Team

Production Manager	**John Titcombe**
Company Stage Manager	**Rickie Gilgunn**
Deputy Stage Manager	**Jane Andrews**
Assistant Stage Manager	**Christine Hollinshead**
Costume Supervisor	**Henrietta Worrall-Thompson**
Deputy Costume Supervisor	**Teri Buxton**
Costume Assistant/Dresser	**Helen Gardner**
Addittional Wardrobe Assistant	**Ros Liddington**
Additional Dresser	**Clare Threadgold**
Set Built By	**Tim Reed, Abe Ahmed and Oliver Ralph**
Set Painted by	**Rod Holt, Sally Holt and Jack Tierney**
Technical Manager	**Barny Meats**
Senior Technicians	**Peter Hunter, Dave Marsh and Mark Noble**
Technicians	**Scott Gurd, Jon Roache and Michael Scott**

The Magna Carta Plays was commissioned and first produced by Salisbury Playhouse on 22 October 2015, in the following order: *Kingmakers, Pink Gin, Ransomed,* and *We Sell Right*

**Original Drama at Salisbury Playhouse.
Supported by Frank and Elizabeth Brenan.**

SALISBURY PLAYHOUSE

Salisbury Playhouse is one of Britain's leading producing theatres, with a national reputation for home-grown work of the highest quality that attracts audiences from across Wiltshire, Hampshire, Dorset and beyond.

The building comprises the 517-seat Main House, the 149-seat Salberg, a purpose-built Rehearsal Room and Community & Education Space. There is also an on-site scenery workshop, wardrobe and props store.

In addition to producing its own productions and welcoming the UK's leading touring companies, Salisbury Playhouse's extensive Take Part programme engages with more than 14,000 people of all ages each year.

The Magna Carta Plays are part of Original Drama, Salisbury Playhouse's commitment to producing new work from and about the South West, which launched in 2014 with the premiere of *Worst Wedding Ever* by *Broadchurch* creator Chris Chibnall.

Artistic Director **Gareth Machin**
Executive Director **Sebastian Warrack**

www.salisburyplayhouse.com

Contents

The scripts went to print before the end of rehearsals and may differ slightly from those presented on stage.

Howard Brenton

RANSOMED

Characters

DETECTIVE INSPECTOR 'ELLIE BAXTER'
(aka 'ANN PEARCE', real name PAT NASH)

POLICE CONSTABLE HAROLD BUDD

MRS MADDELEY COACH
Bishop's housekeeper

CANON SIMON ST JOHN
Cathedral curator

ROGER SYLVESTER
MI5 officer

CAROLINE MONTFICHET
Aristocrat

YURY STANOVICH KOBA
Oligarch

Two non-speaking HEAVIES – playing thieves,
Special Branch men and bodyguards

Setting
In the fictional Cathedral town of Melchester
and nearby countryside

Time
Now

'To no one will we sell,
to no one will we deny or delay,
right or justice'
MAGNA CARTA Clause 40

SCENE ONE

Cathedral. Just before dawn.

CANON SIMON ST JOHN – early 40s, painfully wiry – is stripped to the waist and flogging himself. His clothes are folded neatly beside him on the stage. His dog collar is prominent.

ST JOHN: Soli Deo gloria.

He flogs himself. Yells.

ST JOHN: Soli Deo gloria.

He flogs himself. Yells.

ST JOHN: Soli Deo Gloria.

He flogs himself. Yells. Pauses, out of breath.

ST JOHN: Well someone's got to do it, it's a fallen world.

A very loud alarm goes off.

Two figures – black leather balaclavas, one carrying a silver, flat metal case, run on at the back of the stage. They stop for a moment. ST JOHN looks at them. One of them blows him a kiss and laughs. Then they exit, running.

ST JOHN gathers his clothes hurriedly and exits, stumbling. He leaves the whip behind.

The alarm continues then stops.

Nothing happens for a while.

Then two POLICE FIGURES in white forensic suits and masks enter and approach the whip gingerly.

There are intermittent bursts of incomprehensible police channel chat.

The FIRST POLICE FIGURE photographs the whip. The SECOND opens an evidence bag. The FIRST lifts the whip carefully and puts it in the evidence bag and seals it.

They exit.

SCENE TWO

Bishop's Palace.

Enter DETECTIVE INSPECTOR ELLIE BAXTER and DETECTIVE CONSTABLE BUDD. He sniffs.

BUDD: *(Wiltshire. Sniffs.)* That churchy smell. Mouldy hymn books.

ELLIE: *(South London accent.)* Forensically nosed, are you?

BUDD: I observe, Ma'am.

ELLIE: Do you now. All of Melchester smells of mould to me.

BUDD: Bit of a backwater for you Ma'am, after the London lights?

ELLIE: Don't get lippy, Constable.

BUDD: No Ma'am, sorry. *(A beat.)* But this could be massive.

ELLIE: Up for massive, are you?

BUDD: Too right! Be a media storm, this will! Yeah, bring it on! *(A gesture. A beat.)* Ma'am.

ELLIE sighs.

Enter MRS MADELEY COACH.

COACH: The Canon will be with you shortly, Inspector.

ELLIE: Thank you Ms, Miss …

COACH: Mrs is all I need. This terrible thing!

ELLIE: Our enquiries are …

COACH: Like ripping out the heart of England!

ELLIE: Our enquiries are …

COACH: I mean are we going to have nothing left in this country, nothing that is sacred to us?

ELLIE: Our enquiries are …

COACH: How on earth did they get in? I mean the crypt doors, the timed locks, the alarms … Was anyone hurt?

ELLIE: As far as our enquiries reveal, at this moment in time, no.

COACH: Well that's a blessing, the last thing I wanted. It's the cuts of course.

ELLIE: Right.

COACH: It's not just in hospitals, it's in churches too – the cutting. If England were a forest there'd be no trees left.

BUDD: Sign of the times.

ELLIE glares at him.

COACH: We're a very small cathedral. We can't ring the bells for fear of the spire falling down. I'm chair of 'Ring out again, Melchester', but donations are slow. And there's terrible rot in the choir. But we've got this one glorious attraction, only three copies outside the British Library: Lincoln, Salisbury and us. We get visitors, mostly Americans, Japanese, Russians. I think foreigners love this country more than we do. But now even that has gone.

ELLIE: I assure you we are doing everything to …

COACH: What this is going to do to the Bishop? You see … *(Low.)* He says it's indigestion but I know it's worse.

BUDD: We all fall apart.

COACH: Very true, young man. The Bishop's self control is godly. There're not many saints left in England.

ELLIE: And we are always very grateful for their full co-operation.

MRS COACH suspects sarcasm. ELLIE is impassive.

Enter CANON SIMON ST JOHN. He extends a hand to BUDD.

ST JOHN: *(To BUDD.)* Forgive me, I had to wake His Grace with the terrible news.

COACH: If His Grace is awake I must take him his broth.

She exits.

ST JOHN: *(To BUDD.)* So Inspector, do you have any idea who could be responsible for this outrage?

BUDD stares at him.

ELLIE: This is Detective Constable Budd. I am Detective Inspector Baxter.

ST JOHN: Oh. Gender glitch! Ha!

ELLIE: And you, Sir, are …

ST JOHN: Simon St John, Canon, curator here at Melchester.

ELLIE: Responsible for the missing item.

ST JOHN: The great charter, itself evidence in a crime. So ironic.

ELLIE: Ironic, how?

ST JOHN: Well, it was created in the 13th century to stop crime, establish the rule of law.

ELLIE: And did it?

ST JOHN: No, not really.

ELLIE: So. *(A beat.)* What is it?

ST JOHN: You've not visited our greatest treasure?

ELLIE: No.

ST JOHN: Have you been stationed in Melchester long?

ELLIE: Six months.

ST JOHN: I see. *(A beat.)* Well. As to what it is … it's an agreement, signed in 1215, between King John and the barons of the day, aimed at forcing the King to …

ELLIE: No, no, forget that, what I want to know is exactly what is the object that you have lost?

ST JOHN: That *I* have lost?

EILLIE: Well, looks like a bit of Merrie Olde England has been spirited away right under your nose.

ST JOHN: I don't like your tone, Inspector.

ELLIE: No? Can you roll it up?

ST JOHN: Well you should… roll up that woman's tongue!

They stare at each other.

ST JOHN: I'm sorry, I'm sorry, the shock, the strain. On edge, I … Yes. The charter as mere object. Well, it's a piece of vellum, that is sheepskin, so big… *(Gesture)* … Covered in writing, rather fine writing, done with quill pens in an ink made of oak gall … In the good Lord's name, surely you know what Magna Carta is? Do our police have to be vacant potato heads, ignorant of the country they are meant to be protecting?

ELLIE: Nulli vendemus, nulli negabimus, aut differamus, rectum aut justitiam.

ST JOHN and BUDD stare at her.

ST JOHN: Goodness.

ELLIE: Clause 40 of the charter.

ST JOHN: Indeed.

ELLIE: More important than Clause 39 which people bang on about, wouldn't you think?

ST JOHN: Yes. Yes I would. Where did you learn Latin?

ELLIE: I picked it up, along the way.

ST JOHN: You surprise me.

ELLIE: No one is what they seem. *(A beat.)* So: can you roll it up?

ST JOHN: That would be catastrophic. The vellum is very dry. And without the humidifier installed in the cathedral display, one fears the worse.

ELLIE: So why do you think anyone would steal this … flakey bit of old sheep?

ST JOHN: Your guess is as good as mine.

ELLIE: Is it? *(To BUDD.)* Constable, the …

She nods to him.

BUDD: Yes, Ma'am.

He exits. ELLIE and ST JOHN stand looking at each other.

ST JOHN: What university did you go to?

ELLIE: Who says I did?

ST JOHN: You are hostile.

ELLIE: Aren't I just.

ST JOHN: Why are modern young women so judgmental?

ELLIE: Cos there's a lot out there to judge.

ST JOHN: Someone's got to carry the sins of the world.

ELLIE: Oh yeah? How are you getting on with that, as a priest?

ST JOHN: How are you getting on with it, as a policewoman?

They stare at each other.

CONSTABLE BUDD enters. He has a large plastic evidence bag. ST JOHN's whip is inside it.

ELLIE: This was found in the cathedral.

ST JOHN stares at it.

ELLIE: Can you help us in identifying its nature?

ST JOHN: It is … a devotional object. *(A beat.)* And mine.

ELLIE: The sins of the world on your back?

ST JOHN: That is the general idea.

ELLIE: So you left it in the nave. When?

ST JOHN: This morning.

ELLIE: Did you see the robbery take place?

ST JOHN: *(A beat.)* Yes.

ELLIE: Why didn't you tell us that at once?

ST JOHN: Don't you have an iota of human understanding …

ELLIE: I don't need to understand, I just need to know.
(Nods to BUDD who opens a notebook.) What did you see?

    A doorbell rings offstage.

ST JOHN: Two men. Yes, two.

ELLIE: Can you describe them?

ST JOHN: They … no. They had … *(Gesture over head.)*
Over their heads.

ELLIE: Balaclavas?

ST JOHN: Yes and … they … had a case. A metal, shiny thing.

ELLIE: Big enough for the missing item?

ST JOHN: I would say so, yes.

ELLIE: A special case, made for the job, was it? Maybe with
some kind of humidifier thingy built into it?

ST JOHN: How … could I possibly know that?

    For a moment they are staring at each other. Then COACH enters.

COACH: Canon I'm very sorry but …

ROGER SYLVESTER – fine suit, camel coat … sweeps into the room. Behind him a SPECIAL BRANCH OFFICER.

ROGER: And thank you, Inspector. Canon, would you please step out of the room.

CROUCH exits.

ELLIE: *(Furious.)* Oh for crying out loud …

ROGER: Canon.

ST JOHN: I'm sorry I don't understand …

ROGER: This is now a matter of national security, Canon St John.

ELLIE: This is outrageous!

ROGER: Isn't it, old thing.

ELLIE: Is there paperwork?

ROGER: Don't be silly.

ELLIE: Sod you, Roger!

ROGER: Oh Patricia, Patricia. This is out of your hands now.

He suddenly points his finger into her face, threateningly, arm fully extended.

So do not, just do not. And no media. That's from the highest on high. Total, choking lockdown blackout. Canon, please, with me, now.

ROGER and the SPECIAL BRANCH OFFICER go off with the bewildered ST JOHN.

BUDD: Who was that?

ELLIE: That, Constable, was the deep state.

BUDD: You mean … Oh.

ELLIE: It's all motes of dust in the air.

BUDD: Why would they …

ELLIE: Don't let it worry your pretty little head.

BUDD: But this could be, I mean, mega career leg-up time!

ELLIE: Whatever it is, they won't let a plod like you anywhere near it. Special Branch will do the heavy lifting.

BUDD: But you knew him. And he called you another name …

ELLIE: Harold, it is Harold isn't it? This is my advice: from now on see nothing, hear nothing, think nothing.

BUDD: You spoke Latin.

ELLIE: Oh yeah, highly suspicious. Latin, these days?

BUDD: Well it is a bit iffy.

   She laughs.

BUDD: *(Low.)* Did you work for SIS?

   She turns away.

BUDD: Sorry Ma'am. But I really fancy Special Branch. Maybe you could have a word …

ELLIE: I am a poisoned well, Constable.

BUDD: But we're onto this case. There's someone on the inside, right, and we know who! It's got to be that whipping vicar.

ELLIE: He's not a vicar, he's a canon. And it's not him.

   Enter MRS COACH.

COACH: Inspector, I must protest! I was spooning the Bishop his broth and in bursts that very rude young man. Is he with you?

ELLIE: Not with, more over.

COACH: Chicken soup splattered on the coverlet! 18th century, scenes of the Apostles in a glorious stitch.

ELLIE: Sorry for the stitching but he is my superior.

COACH: Then I can only pity you in your subservience. I will not let this pass. I warn you: the Bishop often makes a four with the Chief Constable.

She turns to go.

ELLIE: The last thing you wanted.

A beat.

COACH: I beg your pardon?

ELLIE: About the robbery. You said it is was a blessing no one was hurt because it was the last thing you wanted.

COACH: One is thankful.

ELLIE: The last thing you wanted when you … did what?

MRS COACH stares at her, suddenly terrified.

ELLIE: That 'rude young man' is from the Secret Intelligence Services. The theft is now a matter of state security. You are out of your depth, my dear. And there are depths in this country into which you do not want to fall.

COACH: We're not living in a police state!

ELLIE: That depends who you are.

A pause.

COACH: I want to hear the bells again. Cathedral bells, the music of England. I want the music of England back. Harmony amongst us.

ELLIE: Sweet singing in the choir.

COACH: Yes. Yes! His Grace the Bishop is dying you know. If only he could hear a peal on a Sunday morning, just once more.

They look at each other.

COACH: I've never done anything dangerous in my life. Ever. Oh sweet Jesus, my Lord, help me.

BUDD: Fat chance o' that!

ELLIE: Constable, get out!

BUDD: But this is a witness, you'll want a corroborated statement …

ELLIE: Piss off, Harold!

BUDD exits, offended.

COACH is in tears.

ELLIE: Person who contacted you, man or woman?

COACH: Woman.

ELLIE: Accent?

COACH: Oh English. One of those pinnacle types.

ELLIE: Pinnacle?

COACH: Shoes and legs that go right up. Tatler trash.

ELLIE: And she, what, turned up on the Palace's doorstep …

COACH: It was in the Cathedral. I heard her shoes behind me, clack clack. I turned round and there she was. Tottering away. Blonde.

ELLIE: What did she say?

COACH: She said … she said she and her fiancé wanted to get married in the cathedral. And what a pity it was about the bells. *(A beat.)* But he was a rich man. Very rich. *(A beat.)* And he could do something about it. *(A beat.)* And the bells would ring out for their wedding.

ELLIE: And then?

COACH: Then she went into a pew and knelt down to pray. Which was a bit of a miracle in that skirt.

ELLIE: Did you meet her again?

COACH, still very frightened, shakes her head.

ELLIE: So there was another contact.

COACH: I was in the Palace's kitchen garden, cutting some greens, the Bishop still likes his greens. And this short, sort of wide man came through the back gate. He was … charming.

ELLIE: Did he have an accent?

COACH: Yes.

ELLIE: S'alright, Maddely. Maddely, isn't it?

MRS COACH nods. ELLIE touches her shoulder.

COACH: He said he'd give it back. He said it was a … a joke.

ELLIE: He promised to pay for the bells?

COACH: He said … there could be untraceable donations.

ELLIE: Oh yeah.

COACH: Who are these people? What do they want with the charter?

ELLIE: What was it you said? Foreigners love this country more than we do?

A moment then the scene is over. ELLIE stays on stage.

SCENE THREE

Cathedral grounds. NB: in this scene ELLIE's accent is middle class.

Enter ROGER.

ROGER: I can't be anywhere near you.

ELLIE: But here you are.

ROGER: It's a matter of toxicity.

ELLIE: Absolutely.

ROGER: I didn't want to know where they'd …

ELLIE: Where they'd thrown me away?

ROGER: Melchester? Jesus.

ELLIE: Well, you've kicked over my stone and here I am.

ROGER: What's with the South London accent? Working a legend for the locals, woman cop fleeing the big bad city?

ELLIE: Something like that.

ROGER: Well I spose we have to be professional about this.

ELLIE: Oh yes, let's.

They stare at each other.

A pause.

ROGER: So who was it on the inside? The holier than thou housekeeper who wants to get into the Bishop's Y-fronts, or the self-loathing, DIY flagellating Canon?

ELLIE: Does it matter? It'll all be hushed up, I imagine?

ROGER: Ours not to reason why.

ELLIE: But I do. It's an outrageous theft, but it looks like a publicity stunt. All that's needed is honest police work, so why are spooks sliming all over us?

He sighs. A beat.

ROGER: Look at the moss on that wall. This town is rotting.

ELLIE: Yes, I've begun to like it. *(A beat.)* This is out of Russia, isn't it?

ROGER: Pat …

ELLIE: Which one's broken cover?

ROGER: Pat …

ELLIE: There are three big bad bears at present on these islands.

ROGER: Pat …

ELLIE: Krushotkin, Nekrassov, Koba. Three old pals of Putin no longer on his Christmas card list who have, so far, avoided a mysterious death. There was a fourth of course but he went by radioactive cheeseburger. Why would an oligarch worth billions eat a cheeseburger? Come to that, why would one want to nick Magna Carta?

ROGER: Do not do this!

ELLIE: Of the three of them, I'd guess Koba.

ROGER: Beulah Road, Pat. *(A beat.)* Beulah Road.

A pause.

ELLIE: Ah, past sins. How they shine on in the here and now.

ROGER: After that catastrophe …

ELLIE: It was not a catastrophe! It was a gross injustice!

ROGER: I'm not going to argy bargy with you. The Cabinet Office wanted you hung, drawn, quartered and buried below high tide. They can still cut you off anytime.

ELLIE: *(To herself.)* Beulah Road.

ROGER: You know you went over the line.

ELLIE: Our masters needn't worry, I'm all for the quiet life.

ROGER: I hope to God you are.

She flicks her hair with her hand.

ELLIE: See? Melchester moss growing in my hair.

She gives a big smile.

ROGER: I mean it 'Ellie'. One twitch and you are dead.

ELLIE: Well.

ROGER: Yes, well.

He is about to go.

ROGER: The canon or the housekeeper?

ELLIE: Neither.

ROGER: You sure?

ELLIE: I am a very good DI.

ROGER: What, you think they hacked in to the cathedral systems, got the codes?

ELLIE: Who am I to say?

ROGER: No one. No one at all. Stay out of our way.

> *He exits. ELLIE stays on the stage for a moment. Then she decides something and exits quickly.*

SCENE FOUR

Army land.

Off, several car doors slam.

Enter two HEAVIES in leather coats, dark glasses. They look around.

Then enter YURY STANOVICH KOBA and CAROLINE MONTIFICHET. They are in elegant country clothes. His coat is commodious.

CAROLINE: Where are we?

YURY: This was a most beautiful English village. But your British Army took the land for a firing range.

CAROLINE: Creepyville, Yury!

YURY: Very creepy. Now it is abandoned because of cuts. But no one comes because of bombs.

CAROLINE: You mean one could tread …

YURY: 'Boom' anytime. Great fun.

> *He stamps and laughs.*

CAROLINE: Maddogsville, Yury!

YURY: Don't worry, darling heart, my people have cleared a path. It is a good place to do business.

CAROLINE: Scare people to death!

YURY: Yes.

CAROLINE: *(Looking around.)* The wild flowers love it.

YURY: Nature is brutal.

A pause.

CAROLINE: So. You want to frighten this woman?

YURY: She asked to meet, I said where.

CAROLINE: Maxyville risky.

YURY: Risk is the spice of life.

CAROLINE: We must make this work. It will work, won't it.

YURY: Everything is possible.

CAROLINE: No rules!

YURY: Oh there are rules. Sadly God has kept them secret from us.

CAROLINE: I go cold when you say God.

YURY: I know, I know. But in His absence someone has to do His job.

He laughs. She embraces him.

CAROLINE: Yury, make them give it to you. You deserve it so much. They don't realize what you've done for the country.

YURY: Don't worry, my sweetness. I will be English.

The HEAVIES react to something. They shield YURY and CAROLINE.

Enter ELLIE. Her accent is now English county.

ELLIE: Do I have the pleasure of speaking to Mr. Yury Stanovich Koba?

A pause as they sum each other up.

YURY: Where is the Bishop's housekeeper?

ELLIE: She is indisposed.

YURY: Unfortunate. What is the nature of her indisposition?

ELLIE: Terror.

YURY: There's a lot of it about.

CAROLINE: I don't like this, Yury, you want the old bag.

ELLIE: Well he's got the young bag instead.

YURY laughs.

YURY: What is your relationship with Mrs Coach?

ELLIE: She's … my aunt.

YURY: *(Snaps.)* She has committed crime! Sold me Cathedral security codes! Now she has terror?

ELLIE: People get scared.

YURY: Of course they get scared! If they didn't, how would I get things done?

He laughs again and relaxes.

YURY: So what does your auntie want?

ELLIE: You to return the charter.

YURY: And why should I do that?

ELLIE: Generosity of spirit?

CAROLINE laughs. YURY is not amused.

YURY: We had a deal. As we talk, sums of money make their way from distant islands like migrating birds. They fly through modern bank systems to your auntie's little charity. These birds cannot be turned back.

ELLIE: Well, good. The money will rebuild the spire.
The bells will ring out. The charter will be back in its case for
the tourists. And you will be married.

A pause.

YURY: Remiss of me. I have not introduced you to my fiancé,
the Right Honorable Caroline Montfichet.

ELLIE: Anne Pearce.

CAROLINE, a little wave of the hand.

CAROLINE: Yah yah, hi hi.

ELLIE: Montfichet, interesting name.

CAROLINE: Dagsville at school.

ELLIE: Richard de Montfichet. One of the barons at
Runnymede. *(A beat.)* A member of the surety. The committee
of twenty-five set up to force the King to keep to the charter.
Any relation?

CAROLINE: They say he owned half of Essex. Thank God we
don't now.

ELLIE: So your fiancé's name gave you the idea for the theft?

YURY: Despite the centuries her DNA may still be on the
parchment. What better wedding gift for my bride?

ELLIE: Romantic.

YURY: I am incurable. Will we make the front cover of
Country Life?

ELLIE: Maybe the front door of Belmarsh Prison.

YURY squints.

YURY: You … You … you are not the Bishop's sad
housekeeper's niece. Come, come, Anne Pearce, as the saying
goes: 'it takes one to know one?'.

A moment, both still.

YURY: But you are not my contact.

ELLIE: I outrank him.

CAROLINE: You outrank Roger?

YURY: Caroline.

CAROLINE: This woman is crapazollering us around.

YURY: My love, shut up your pretty mouth.

CAROLINE: Jesusville!

She turns away.

YURY: So.

He takes the charter out of his coat. It is rolled up. ELLIE flinches.

YURY: Yes, it rolls up. My experts said it wouldn't.

ELLIE: So did ours.

YURY: See? *(He shakes it out.)* It is very flexible. As it has been politically, for eight hundred years.

ELLIE: The British Government will not do what you want.

YURY: No?

He squints again.

YURY: There is something wrong about you. Caroline has excellent instincts about other women.

CAROLINE: She's a phoneyvilletime two-faced bitch.

YURY: See what I mean?

CAROLINE: I need a bath, a real fire and a drink, so kill her or something, Yury.

YURY: There speaks the Baron's descendant.

ELLIE: You want British citizenship and a British passport. You offered the Government two million pounds to become

British. Other oligarchs have gone that route, but you the Home Office turned down.

YURY: If only the British were wholehearted in their corruption, the country would work so much better.

ELLIE: You are desperate.

YURY: I am. For liberty.

ELLIE: A passport for Magna Carta.

YURY: 'Tasty' is the word, no?

ELLIE: The government will never agree.

YURY: They agreed for others. Two million pounds is a reasonable price.

ELLIE: For you, I suppose, the cost of a good haircut.

YURY: Do not cheek, Miss Ann, or whoever you are. They turned me down. But why? Countrymen of mine own most of your Hampstead and your London Mayfair and your Gloucestershire, and one third of Scotland. We take over your stately homes! We manage your big estates! We care for your countryside! We mend your hedgerows, we revive your fox huntings! We are the barons now!

CAROLINE: Don't rant, Yury, you know what happens when you rant …

YURY: I will rant! *(Waves Magna Carta.)* Why do you think this document has anything to do with democracy?

ELLIE: It made us all equal under the law.

YURY: Bullshite!

ELLIE: It laid the seed of Parliamentary democracy.

YURY: Bull shitey shitey shitey nonsense! It's aim was to seize power from a mad tyrannical president – I mean king. And give it to an elite. The barons. And we are their heirs. You and I, Miss Ann, we are the elite: I the business man, you the secret police. All the democratic flim-flam, your shoutings in your Westminster Commons, your Today programme trick questionings, your first past the postings, your polls and ballot votings, all a veneer. A slime that has set hard over the truth about power. Democracy is the fooling of the many by the few. And I say thank God.

He calms down then holds up Magna Carta.

This little bit of paper gave power to us, Ann. We, the secret masters and mistresses. Yes, we are the barons.

ELLIE: You will never get a British passport.

YURY: No?

ELLIE: And in the end we will freeze your bank accounts, confiscate your estates.

YURY: *(Laughs.)* What? A leftwing secret policeman? That is a phenomenon totally unknown.

ELLIE: Really? Didn't you have them in Russia once? Weren't you one, Yury Stanovich?

A pause.

YURY: Whoever you are, you and I could do wonders.

ELLIE: No passport.

YURY: OK.

He tears Magna Carta, taking some time, into pieces and throws them up into the air.

They all stare down at the pieces.

CAROLINE: Oh sodsuckssville, Yury! This kind of thing happens when you rant!

YURY: Yes. *(Looks at the pieces around him.)* Interesting.

Enter fast ROGER with COACH and ST JOHN. The two HEAVIES draw hand guns. COACH and ST JOHN are distressed.

COACH: I had to tell him where you were going to …

ST JOHN: *(Sees the torn parchment.)* What is that?

ROGER: *(To ELLIE.)* Patricia, this time …

COACH: *(To ELLIE.)* I am so sorry …

ST JOHN: He's torn it up! He's torn up the great charter!

ROGER: That is unfortunate, Mr. Koba. I was authorized to tell you: a passport would be yours, in exchange.

KOBA: Ah. Well, we may yet come to an arrangement. Roger, speak privately. *(Looks at ELLIE.)* Away from this person, whoever she may be.

ROGER: I can assure you, Yury Stanovich, she is absolutely no one.

ROGER, KOBA, CAROLINE and the two HEAVIES exit.

COACH: Quick, pick up the bits before they get soggy!

ST JOHN: Yes, restoration! They can do miracles. Digitalise the joins …

ELLIE: Maybe it's best torn up.

He stops and stares at her.

ST JOHN: You people, the lot of you running and ruining this country, are you all vandals? Don't you care? Look!

He points at a fragment in his hand. Reads.

ST JOHN: '… pro nobis et heredibus nostris in perpetuum, omnes libertates subscriptas.'

ELLIE: 'For us and our heirs forever, all the liberties written below …'

A beat.

ELLIE: 'Course I care about our liberties. We need a new Magna Carta. The trouble is … Who's going to write it?

ST JOHN: Perhaps it's best written in our hearts.

ELLIE: That's too deep for me, Canon.

ST JOHN: Really? I think not.

He looks at the fragment. He lets it fall to the ground.

A silence.

COACH: His Grace The Bishop. *(Stops.)* His Grace the Bishop. *(Stops.)* His Grace the Bishop has a very fine 25 year-old Macallan malt whisky.

They look at her.

COACH: Perhaps a small stiffener?

ST JOHN: That could be appropriate. Inspector, perhaps you …

ELLIE: Oh, I think so.

End of play.

Anders Lustgarten

KINGMAKERS

Characters

LORD LAMPREY

DUKE VENAL

LADY PLUNDER

EARL GRABBER

SPROCKET

1225. England. A luxurious dining hall in a baron's palace. Feasting at the table are the assembled peers of England, clad in silks, furs and jewelled finery. Among them: LORD LAMPREY, DUKE VENAL, LADY PLUNDER, EARL GRABBER, and sundry divers others. Standing discreetly in the shadows, watching them with some distaste, is SPROCKET, a man of poor birth risen to be advisor to LAMPREY. He is sombrely dressed and holds a copy of the Magna Carta. He steps forward and addresses us.

SPROCKET: My name is Sprocket, and my function's same:
I wheel the deals of bigger cogs than I.
Though small in size, my turning gear will make
Wheels crunch, their axles spin, and burdens shift.
Though scarcely known among the men I serve,
Many of whom can't quite recall my name,
Machines don't work without me. Parts don't start.
And noble ranks, of pomp and circumstance,
Throw up their arms and look for someone poor
To blame. Or fix it. Either way. No odds.
Gold pays for words their wits refuse to shape
And crafts delights their hands could never make.
But there we are. Of me, in brief, let's say:
I am a man who turns the world my way.
And like all cogs, two things give me most peace:
Sharp teeth, and generous supply of grease.

Let's take advantage of this antique style
To bring you up to date with where we are.
It is the year of twelve and twenty-five.
Ten years ago, these Barons I do serve
Did cut a deal with John, their loathsome king,
To divvy up the ruling class's loot.
It's fair to say that in the press release
That's not how they described their little coup.
They lauded it the triumph of liberty!
The ripping down of monarchy's dead shroud!
A move from dark and tyrannous night to bright
And shining freedom's day, where rights and powers
Did wax and grow like glorious summer flowers
Released from brutal winter's frigid grip.

That last bit's mine. It's how I earn my keep.
I sell my wit for dear, and honour cheap.

Not long thereafter, John mysteriously died
(Before you ask, we all have alibis)
And left his young son Henry in the care
Of William Marshal, Regent, hard but fair.
Who, thank the Lord, has gone to meet his Lord
Which lets them now put Henry to the sword.
That's why this boisterous roistering's happening here:
To mark a royal dispatch drawing near.
For when the young pretender's out the way
This vulpine lot will have untrammelled sway.

An argument breaks out at the table.

VENAL: Which of you scum has purchased Hertfordshire?

GRABBER: Don't look at me.

LAMPREY: Nor I.

VENAL: Then who?

PLUNDER: 'Tis mine!

VENAL: Fuck you!

PLUNDER: Tough cheese, old bean. Hard lines. Is that
How English people talk? I think 'tis so.
A Norman noble finds it hard to master
England's incomprehensible vernacular.

VENAL: I've had my eye upon that spot for time.
But had to squeeze the cash out of my peasants.

LAMPREY: Don't call them that. We did discuss. Not smart.

VENAL: Who cares? In closèd chamber we need not
Stop our mouths. But how –

PLUNDER: With foreign finance swift sought out, I bought
That bounteous county's fields and streams and roads,
To bar the way to ravening hordes of poor

Which now upon its bounties feast for free.
In future years, should peasants want to drink,
Or farm, or walk, they'll have to pay.

LAMPREY: Subjects!

PLUNDER: Whatever.

VENAL: You bitch. That deal was mine.

A brawl breaks out, with lots of shouting and shoving.

SPROCKET: They're not a charming bunch, I have to say.
Lamprey, my master, like that sucking fish
Which lately brought demise upon King John,
Doth drain the life and vital force from men.
His cohorts, Venal, Grabber, Plunder, all
Like licentious philanderers masked at ball,
They swing from grasp to grasp, from haunt to haunt,
Looking to see who'll give them what they want.
Charming as leprosy, gracious as the grave,
This is the class which owns this country now.
Their banquet has that nasty edge which comes
From being one up on someone else. The foolish
Would-be king believes this noble feast
Is held to mark ascension to his throne.
This lot believe he'll play the Banquo role.
But I in turn must make this story whole.

He steps from the shadows and addresses the brawling throng.

My lords! Gentlemen! My nobles! AHEM!

They turn and vengefully take his presence in.

VENAL: Who's this now? That dares disrupt our sport?

LAMPREY: My retainer. Springet is his name.

SPROCKET: Sprocket, sir.

LAMPREY: Though short –

SPROCKET: I'm average height.

LAMPREY: He's smart with cash.

VENAL: How nice.

SPROCKET: My lord, your kindness makes a splash.

GRABBER: Hush your mouth, you sarky little twat,
And still your tongue, else see it loll and flop
Salted and chilled upon a plate for lunch. Mmmmm.

SPROCKET: *(Aside.)* Looking at him, I would not guess
Another meal to be his greatest need.

GRABBER: What?

SPROCKET: Good sir, please know, my sole intent
Is saving you from harsh predicament.

GRABBER: What does he mean? Predicament there's none!

SPROCKET: It's called democracy, monsieur.

GRABBER: Eh?

SPROCKET: And tax.

PLUNDER: Fuck me, is English hard!
I've sat for hours, hunched o'er my books piled tall,
But neither word rings any bells at all!

GRABBER: Tax is the thing the little people pay
To fund the noble privilege of our stay.
The other thing's all Greek to me.

LAMPREY: Good friends, we must confront a brutal truth.
We are not popular. In fact, we're hated.
Our towering castles, built at great expense,
Loom high above the hovels of the poor.
Our copious feasting lodges in their craw.
Our sumptuous robes, our carriages of gold,
Consumption that bespeaks a life of ease.
For poor, consumption's merely a disease.

PLUNDER: Our function's simple: we inspire! Perchance
The common man looks up at us and thinks
"One day I'll be like them!"

SPROCKET: *(Aside.)*   He's got no chance.

PLUNDER: And back he turns to worthy toil and graft.
And thus we decent men create from knaves.

SPROCKET: *(Aside.)* Whose sole reward is sleep in early graves.

LAMPREY: You miss the point.
It's not the wealth that hacks them off. It's not
The sprawling piles or endless holidays.
It's broken promises. We said, when we
Took power from king, we'd open up these new
Found rights to all mankind to be enjoyed.

PLUNDER: And so we did!

LAMPREY: Er, not so much.
(He takes the Magna Carta from SPROCKET and quotes from it.)
"No man to be arrested or imprisoned,
Outlawed, exiled, in any way destroyed,
Save by the lawful judgement of his peers."

PLUNDER: Ah. Ooops. Missed that bit.

LAMPREY: "To no-one will we sell, to none delay,
Rights or justice."

GRABBER: *(Looking.)* There are no footnotes there?
Exceptions?

LAMPREY: There aren't.

GRABBER: Not e'en for those
We can accuse betray our state abroad?
Who go unto the Middle East to fight
Religious wars, crusades, conflicts of faith?
We may not lock them up? For public health?

LAMPREY: This text says no.

VENAL: Then let it burn to ash.
As now it has. Our late and unlamented former king
Did have it quashed by papal intercede
Mere months beyond the deal at Runnymede.

45

Its work is done. In years come after
Who'll remember Magna Carta?

LAMPREY: The point is this:
Those crimes of which we did accuse the king
And held above his head to cast a light
Disfavourable and tyrannous 'pon his face,
We now do ourselves! John raised his levies,
Grievous and oppressive as they were,
To fund an army, fight in France,
Restore the heady scent of empire to our land.
(He lost, but hey, at least he tried. And why
We need an empire to have pride
Is for another time)
We take men's tithes to buy luxurious clothes
And shining jewels, like worthless sybarites.
We nothing give to nation, merely take.
Or so it is alleged by Common Man.

VENAL: And so? Have we not weapons, guards and flame?
The military might of conquering power?
What care we that these peasant scum resent
Our sumptuous sovereignty and reign?
What can they do? Who now grips England's balls?
The dukes and lords, with money and with swords.
Us. We are the state now. Money is power.
You don't agree? Detained within the hour.

LAMPREY: That's one approach. For which we have the means.
But Sprocket proffers gentler, more melodic themes.
(To SPROCKET.) Speak.

SPROCKET: The knotty matter's this: you all are frauds.

Rage among the nobles.

GRABBER: Now do I feel that threatened snack enforced:
Ill-mannered tongue beslabbered with special sauce.

SPROCKET: Mistake me not. I speak not my own mind
But that of all your subjects, whose hot rage
And fiery anger turns upon the schism

'Tween those who should have rights and those who get 'em.
Full half the men of England see no boon
From what this vaunted treaty claims to give.
The villeins of this state, the men and women
Who do base work and labour in your fields,
Receive no rights at all. If it's your whim
To turn them off or someway dispossess
Them of their homes and livelihoods, they have
No recompense nor choice but to submit.

PLUNDER: Let me the simple logic of this give:
It's called an economic incentive.
The average worker's lazy, thick, and steals.
Why should we pay for un-entitled meals?

GRABBER: We must be lean and mean and so compete
Or suffer economic cruel defeat.
Our aptest tool to best our foes, you see,
Is labour market flexibility.

SPROCKET: I heartily concur, and would not stop
The rise of business to the very top.
The problem's this: resentment of my lords
Stirs up enraged antagonistic ire.
There are three ways to overcome this flaw.
Repression's one. The second is to grant
Rights full and true to all who populate
This land, the women too.

VENAL draws his sword.

                                    I'll take that as
A No. That leaves us number three, which is
A subtler answer, twisty as a snake.
Take all this strident rage and turn to joy
Where people flood the streets to clap not burn.
In place of scowling faces conjure smiles
And ballèd fist unclench to waving hand.

PLUNDER: Sounds great.

GRABBER: But how?

SPROCKET: Bring back the King.

Consternation and hubbub among the nobles. VENAL waves his sword at SPROCKET.

VENAL: Have you full lost the plot? For one, he is
A *child* of bare eighteen, hapless and weak.
What man would cheer for him? For two, have you
A clue how hard we've scrapped for ten long years
To get these royal fuckers off our backs?
His dipshit dad was tough enough to shift,
His Regent pain in the behind, and now
Just as he reaches his majority
And we can slip some hemlock in his food
(Eighteen's the proper age to poison kings
Go younger and the history books are harsh)
You want to put him back above our heads
And undo all the graft we have put in?

SPROCKET: When were you last beloved? When there was King.

That stops them in their tracks. Pause as they think about it.

For every farm you took, King John stole two.
What monies you did swallow, he took double.
However deep into the trough you dipped,
He shoved his snorting snout yet further in.
Your own delinquencies were overlooked
In light of kingly gross indulgent greed.
And as an ugly man when sat with leper
Doth manage by the contrast to look fair,
So did your lordships in the public eye
Wax bountiful and generous as our Lord.

GRABBER: I see where he doth lead. 'Tis like in form
To when a group commits a robbery.
One fellow's often set in front to fool
The armoured men whose job is staunch defence,
With japes or noise distract them from their task,
While others ransack treasury at will.

PLUNDER: Is that how's done?

GRABBER: I would not know.

PLUNDER: Nor I.
I'm merely asking for a friend.

VENAL: Set up
This royal stripling as new king? Make of
His dim and pretty face a mask to hide
Our own true ugly nature, and distract
Attention from our wanton shameful acts?
Then make him sign a Magna Carta making
Us the Magna? Interesting.
(Beat. He puts his sword away.) I may
Not kill you after all. Go on. How would
We tell this new un-sceptred isle they've been
Re-sceptred?

SPROCKET: The English are a doleful race,
Uncertain who they are. They spit their bile
At immigrants new landed 'pon their shores
Who rob them (so they say) of old traditions.
And yet the king they claim they have been called
"Politically incorrect" to cheer
Is immigrant himself! They *yearn* to turn
The clock back on their own society.
Bend knee, tug forelock, humbled and debased
Before a golden throne, and so relieve
Their frightened spirits of the awful load
That actual freedom places on the spine.
They're spineless. You'll have no problem there.

PLUNDER: What of the Scots and Welsh?

SPROCKET: You'll have to kill them. They have balls.

LAMPREY: It may take time. And swords. We have
Them both. My lords, list close. There's more.

SPROCKET: When formerly you signed that treaty bold,
Your adversary was a slippery eel,
A cunning fox, a haughty eagle high.
Now John is dead, and in his place there stands

A new-fledged chick, his feathers damp with egg.
He nothing knows of politics, that dark
And stormy long night of the soul, whereby
Control's achieved, accounts are fixed. Let's speak
Of gold: he'll need a ton, to fund his own
Strange misadventures here and o'er in France,
Where sultry empire croons her loony tune
Like fatal Circe's song. Who's got gold? You.
You strike a deal, he'll cede authority
Greater than any which now to you befalls.
He'll wear the crown. You'll be the king. That's all.

PLUNDER: How do we know this puppet king plays ball?

SPROCKET: Ask him yourselves. He's waiting in the hall.

An approving hubbub. The nobles intrigue among themselves. Pause.

VENAL: Send him in.

SPROCKET bows and withdraws to the antechamber beyond the hall. The nobles huddle into a welcoming committee, plastering on sickening rictus smiles. SPROCKET returns with a swaggering teenager, HENRY III. The nobles bow sycophantically.

LAMPREY: Your Royal Highness, welcome. On behalf
Of England's noblest gentry gathered here,
On your exalted visage may we wish
The glow of noble Apollo's fiery steed,
The sun herself, may shine, and bring –

HENRY III: Whatever, fam. Your chat is long. I have
Got untold tings I need to do. To make
Me wait's a liberty! You get me, blood?

PLUNDER: *(Sotto voce to nobles.)* What language does he speak?
                                    It is not French,
Nor English from the books I have perused.

HENRY looks admiringly round at the sumptuous dining hall.

HENRY III: Your yard is off the chain though, bruv! Whose crib?

SPROCKET: *(To nobles.)* He complements your chamber, and inquires
To whom it may belong.

LAMPREY: It is mine own.

HENRY holds out a fist for LAMPREY to bump. LAMPREY looks baffled.

HENRY III: My don! Your shit is tight! But why you keep
These sidemen here on lock? Where are the yats?

LAMPREY: The who?

HENRY III: The yats, hot chicks, the fit to hit
It, yeah? It is a partay up in here!

SPROCKET: He wonders –

VENAL: Yes, I know. I have a son
Not far in age who speaks in similar tone.
From what I can discern, it is the speech
Of streets, not he upon the threshold of the throne.

HENRY III: I speak the tongue of bredrins at the club.
That's where my true skills lie: as a DJ.
Next week I drop the mandolin remix
Of Auld Lang Syne. You *know* that shit will bang.

He does a hip hop dance.

LAMPREY: My lord, perhaps a drink? To quench your thirst?

HENRY III: An epic fail. *You* drink.

GRABBER: *(Sotto voce to nobles.)*   'Tis shame he's not
Exact as dim as language makes him sound.

*LAMPREY picks up a flagon from the banquet tables and drinks deeply
from it. He hands the flagon to HENRY, who drinks with enthusiasm.*

LAMPREY: Drink up, Your Highness. Please don't stint. There's more.

HENRY drinks again.

HENRY III: Hear what, when you give me my crown, I'll wear
It in a different style. Like, back to front?

I saw it in a woodcut sent from France.
The shit is sick.

LAMPREY: I doubt it not, though do
Not know the meaning to be good or bad.
Yet look now, Highness, to that very theme:
Ascension to the gilded throne of state.

HENRY III: My birthright and my role when come of age.
As I am now. Today. You feel me, fam?

LAMPREY: Well, yes and no.
I'm sure your honoured Regent did make clear
Before his much lamented death –

HENRY III: It's odd
You say it made you sad: I don't recall
One of your faces at his funeral.

PLUNDER: We did send flowers.

HENRY III: Big whoop.

VENAL: *(To nobles.)* This cocky twat
Does not perceive the way the balance shifts.
It's time for nasty, less of nice. *(To HENRY.)* My lord.
You will not get the Crown. We fought too long,
Against the depredations and excess
Of your benighted pa, to hand the keys
To noble kingdom to his half-formed sprog.

HENRY III: I'm not my dad. You can't blame me for his
Mistakes.

VENAL: Why not? It's only being his son
That puts you in the frame to wear the crown!
What other skills do you possess? Fuck all!
I see your future: gap year off, then join
The army, long way off. The dumping ground
For thick and privileged since dawn of time.

HENRY III: I don't feel well. This drink's too strong. I'm used
To Breezers. Five percent. I must sit down.

He sits heavily in a chair. His façade has gone.

GRABBER: You fancy that? A stint abroad? Amidst
The dust and blood of misbegotten wars?

PLUNDER: Or do the things the normals do to eat:
To have to get a *job*? Or e'en the fate
Accompanying the useless fallen nags
Who lose the kingly race? To be put down?

The nobles draw their fingers across their throats. HENRY retches.

HENRY III: I think I'll puke.

LAMPREY: Not there!

GRABBER: Too late.

HENRY pukes copiously onto the carpet.

SPROCKET: *(Aside.)* The least right fact I ever learned at school?
It's *class* that lets the ruling classes rule.

LAMPREY: *(Angrily to SPROCKET.)* That Turkey carpet is brand new.
                                       If puke
Does not come out or scheme does fail, you'll pay.

SPROCKET: Fear not, my lord. The hook is in. 'Tis now
The time to reel the fish onto the shore.
(He sits HENRY up and passes him some water.)
My lord, sit up. A drink. Of water. Clear
The head. You know, it doesn't have to be
That bad. You can still rule.

HENRY III: *(Pointing at VENAL.)* But that man there –

SPROCKET: A rash impetuous blunt ignoble noble
Is the Duke. Oft times he knows not where
His mouth doth lead. Pay him no heed, I swear.

HENRY III: How can I rule without consent of peers?

SPROCKET: A thing called Magna Carta ring a bell?

HENRY III: The charter Dad knocked on the head? I did
Not think it was that big a deal.

SPROCKET: 'Tis not.
A bagatelle. Yet that by which you will
Gain friendship of these Barons gathered here.
You'll make these knights of honour bend the knee.
Great England's serried ranks of high-born men
Doff cap, defer, acknowledge you in place.
As he whose glow enlightens all our stars,
Our blazing sun, true monarch of our hearts,
Our King!

HENRY: I am!!

SPROCKET whips out a new version of the Magna Carta and holds it aloft.

SPROCKET: Then SIGN!

The new Magna Carta is a lot longer than the old one. It trails to the floor. HENRY looks doubtfully at it. Pause.

HENRY III: It is. Quite long.

SPROCKET hands it to him, pointing out a part.

SPROCKET: Quick skim should do. The germane chapter for
Your eyes is this: that gives you lots of cash.

HENRY reads. Contentment among the nobles. Pause.

HENRY III: I must confess I do prefer to have
My reading stuff engravèd with hot chicks
And know not well the grand affairs of state.
Yet seems all powers and ingots go to you.

SPROCKET: Uh. Oh.

HENRY III: And none to poor. Not that I care. But seems
You take the rights my father used to have
And aggregate them to yourselves, without
Fulfilling promises you've made to men
Of ordinary rank. Or am I wrong?

SPROCKET: *(To nobles.)* It seems we've under-estimated him.
Now does this gormless poshboy fool

Begin to show a smarter, wiser side.
He seeks to cut a better deal for self
And frame it like he's doing us a turn.

VENAL: *(To HENRY.)* Shut trap, get pen, sign name. It's growing late.
Unless you're keen on grim mysterious fate.

HENRY III: But seems to me, my Duke, that if you wished
Me swim with fish, I'd already be paddling.
What could you want of me, a lad not twenty?
Ah!
There is but one of king: of nobles, plenty.

MAJOR muttering and concern among the nobles.

VENAL: *(To SPROCKET.)* You've screwed the pooch. He sees the scheme.
And I'll
Screw you if you don't sort this matter out.

SPROCKET: Good Duke, but stay your ire, I'll bet you'll see
You have good cause to thank not threaten me.

HENRY III: Don't get me wrong. I have no love for those
With whom I've passed the time in bars and clubs.
We lounged like lads, had proper bantz, but all
It was was mere distraction. Now's the time
Like Henries yet to come, to shrug off plebs
And peasants, take my place in pantheon
Of glittering absolutist kings beloved.
The tsar's the star in England, so they say.
My fear is how to do it, given Dad.
His darker deeds; the promises you made.
The English people do not trust your type
Nor mine. We must do something. Make concession.

SPROCKET: *(Aside.)* Now it is clear John gives him ancestry.
The apple does not fall far from the tree.

PLUNDER: You cannot mean we must fulfil what's in
The Magna Carta for the mass? I'm ill
At very thought!

HENRY III: Fear not: though like all kings I am derived
From shallow gene pool, yet I have not dived
Into its deep end and concussed my head.
You may allay your well-entitled dread.
Such policy would nakedly be dense
The cost in power and cash beyond immense.
The trick is this: *distract* the people from
The promises you've made to them. Allay
Their new-found hopeful expectations of
A better, happier, less cruel world to come.

GRABBER: But how?

Pause. HENRY III smiles.

HENRY III: There is one thing in England trumps all else:
A royal wedding.

The nobles break into huge smiles and mutual congratulations.

VENAL: The kid is good.

LAMPREY: I told you so.

VENAL: You did.

SPROCKET: In fact 'twas me.

VENAL: *(Pushes SPROCKET away.)* Shut up and let me hear.

HENRY III: In slack moments inside strip joints, I did
Read up upon the history of kings.
(I hid the book inside some porn. It does
Not do to look too smart). Time after time,
There was a panacea for discontent.
It stopped rebellion in its tracks, assuaged
The sharpest hurts of grim austerity,
Made men forget they could not feed their kids.
It was, of course, the wedding of a prince
To beauteous blushing bride, oft-times princess,
Or even commoner (though *really* posh)
To give the average Joe a sense of hope.
It's quite remarkable the strong effect

A royal wedding has upon the minds
Of men and women (God's grace, the women! Obsessed
With dress and nails and hair and all that shit)
Who think themselves of independent mind.
They all melt down to dribbling pools of goo
Who burble "Majesty" at every turn,
As if somehow their family's hopes and fears
Were sublimated into ours. I guess
They are, if only in the sense we spunk
Their taxes on our fripperies, and so
Take food directly from their kids' own mouths.
The more we get, the less they have: of hope
And power, education, food, the lot.
And yet they love it. Stand and cheer. Seems wrong.
It mystifies me why they go along.

VENAL: They do. That's all. The ones that don't, we'll call
Unpatriotic and a threat to state.
We'll lock them up and say they're driven by
Irrational and misbegotten hate.
Agreed?

HENRY III: Agreed. How like you then my plan?

VENAL, LAMPREY and the rest of the nobles kneel. SPROCKET doesn't.

LAMPREY: Most Royal Highness, please forgive our ways
Untimely, crude and foolish as they are.
We thought you'd be a puppet on a string.
Now do we see the strings you pluck are ours.
Let us from now on be your mandolin
And let us make sweet music all together!

The nobles cheer as one.

PLUNDER: Enthusiastically we do accept
Your proposition of a royal wedding.
And let me swift propose a perfect match:
My own beloved girl shall be your bride!

GRABBER: When she doth say she'll eat a horse, she means

It literally. She weighs a ton. Now *my* –

PLUNDER punches GRABBER.

PLUNDER: You nasty man!

The nobles cluster round HENRY, waving woodcuts of their daughters in his face.

VENAL: My daughter is for miles
Around renowned for beauty unsurpassed.

LAMPREY: She also could not spell a word like 'cat'
If gifted with the c and with the t.
My own fair child –

HENRY III: Enough! There is no lack
Of time to find the lucky lady who'll
Be fortunate enough to bear my heirs.
Cos that's the thing, good Barons, don't forget.
The marriage is the porn flick, but the key,
The money shot? The *kids*. The final nail
In independent England's rotten coffin.
You think a wedding makes 'em bow and cringe?
Just wait until we show our first-born son.

The nobles cheer.

With that in mind, come, let's away and send
For shots of hotties all round Europe, then
As with a medieval Tinder, swipe
To left until we find the one that's right.

They all begin to move off. HENRY raises the new Magna Carta.

One issue left. This thing will have to change.
Returning power and fiscal wealth
My way. An equal partnership requires
An equal share.

The nobles look at each other for a moment, then acquiesce.

But worry not. We'll dump
The worst effects on bad old Dad and make
The history books record it as his shame.

We'll share the cash; he and the people, blame.

They all move off triumphantly, KING HENRY III at their head. SPROCKET manages to catch LAMPREY's arm just before he exits.

SPROCKET: Sir, what of me?

LAMPREY: What of you?

SPROCKET: All I did
To bring this reconciliation on,
And solve your pressing woes, does not deserve
A little something?

Beat. LAMPREY grudgingly pulls out a bag of gold. SPROCKET's eyes light up. LAMPREY reaches inside and pulls out a single gold piece. He hands it over.

LAMPREY: A little something. As you asked.

He laughs contemptuously and exits after the rest. Beat. SPROCKET sits mid-stage, single coin in hand, contemplating it like Hamlet with Yorick. Pause.

SPROCKET: Why do we do it? When we know full well
The rich are turds? What full and deep contempt
They hold us in? They laugh at us from yachts.
It's not their thievery, their cruelty, e'en
Their clear intent to turn the real life clocks
Back to this era we do play. It's what
They make us do to us. A smarter man
Than me once said, just as no two objects
Can in one time take up one single space,
So must one mode of life squeeze out the rest,
Must choke at source the vital oxygen
From other ways of life that seek to breathe.
So does our love of rich asphyxiate
Our thoughts of better, fairer, happier worlds.
There are right now, you may have seen, a rash
(I use the word advisedly) of plays
And books and films about the royals, which make
These hapless plastic twats into great figures

Of weight and moral dignity and power,
Shakespearian in scope. A joke. At time
When elites want our cash and power, it seems
They also want our *sympathy.* The rub:
Where are such tender ministrations for
The ones they rob? The normal men? The poor?
It's propaganda for austerity.
If you can't see that, rather you than me.

Beat. He stands.

And yet I am no better man, of course.
I've made my bundle from the same discourse.
If bundle it be called.

He throws the coin to an audience member.

Here, take, and spend.
Or maybe save. By time that lot in there
Are done, you'll need it for some healthcare for
Your mum. What can we do, eh? Something *better.*
Shrug off this worthless lot, and selves unfetter.

He bows to the audience and strides off in the opposite direction to the one the nobles exited. End of play.

Timberlake Wertenbaker

WE SELL RIGHT

"Things are going to slide in all directions
Won't be nothing
Nothing you can measure anymore..."
Leonard Cohen: The Future.

An old couple, a young girl. The old couple can be two women or a man and a woman. The age is internal. There's plenty of energy.

A feeling of echo and vast space (we could be in a cathedral) but the couple seem bound by their own space. Perhaps a blanket or two. The girl tests the space. She has some kind of mobile.

There's a marked difference between the girl's presence and that of the old couple. Perhaps as simple as age.

— indicates a change of voice between the couple.

GIRL:
They could be listening

COUPLE:
— no one's listening
— not anymore

GIRL:
I was followed

COUPLE:
— sanctuary

GIRL:
What?

She looks at her phone, shakes her head.

COUPLE:
— safety from pursuit or persecution
— a place for injured animals
— holy. For now

GIRL: *(Looks at her phone.)*
I don't have holy

COUPLE:
— deserving special respect

GIRL:
As in respect the rules.
It was a long way
I'm not used to
even allowed
I don't have much time

COUPLE:
— it's been such a long time

GIRL:
I came. Did she – ?
Is she – ?

COUPLE:
— we asked you to come
— begged you
— no, not begged, entreated
— persuaded
— enticed
— lured even.

GIRL: *(Checking phone.)*
I have lured:
temptation

COUPLE:
— or attraction
— to see you
— once more
— before

GIRL:
Is she?
Where?

COUPLE:
— where to start?
— Start at the beginning.

GIRL:
The beginning?

(She checks her phone.)

Origin, source, mainspring, embryo or germ?

COUPLE:
— mainspring
— embryo

GIRL:
Me?

COUPLE:
— You and –

GIRL:
Her?

COUPLE:
— it was the time of the debt
— it was because of the debt.
— No, it started before, long before.
— There was still a debt. There wasn't a surplus.
— I don't think there was much of a debt at the beginning.

GIRL:
We still have debt. I know the word.

COUPLE:
— it can't be worth much.
— Things had to be sold. Because of the debt.
— Before the debt too. Coal. Steel. Railways. Oil.
— Gas, electricity, the post office. That was during the debt.
— Water. Air.
— Air came much later. During the rebellion.

GIRL: *(Checks her phone.)*
Rebellion?

COUPLE:
— civil war

GIRL:
I have war

COUPLE:
— we called it the rebellion.

GIRL:
You can't just call anything anything you want.

COUPLE:
— a rebellion is a decision
— us against them
— us against us.
— No, that's a civil war. We were still us then, they were them
— we thought we were but we weren't
— we were already being sold

GIRL:
She was?

COUPLE:
— when the great sell-off began
— continued, it had been going on.
— Houses. Buildings. Streets. Parks.
— The rebels countered
— they were called protestors then.

GIRL:
Protestor?

COUPLE:
— when you don't agree

GIRL:
Everyone agrees

COUPLE:
— they didn't then
— protests on Hampstead Heath.
— Wilderness. Paths. Rights of way: sold.
— Walk-ins along the Pennine Way.
— Then streets. Pavements.

GIRL:
There were pavements for all?

COUPLE:
— of course. And parks
— castles. Vaults. Monuments. Graveyards
— drum-ins for the graveyards, wake up the dead
— churches, cathedrals
— lie-ins in Lincoln, Durham, Canterbury.
— No, not Canterbury. Canterbury was already sold.
— Perhaps not cathedrals anyway
— I remember cathedrals and churches. Even museums.

GIRL:
Museum?

COUPLE:
— as in private gallery but for everyone.

GIRL: *(Checking her phone.)*
I don't have museum.

COUPLE:
— a building set apart for study or the arts.

GIRL:
Like University

COUPLE:
— but for everyone. For the public. Free.

GIRL: *(Checking her phone.)*
Free?

COUPLE:
— Free. You have free. Surely you have free.

GIRL:
It blinks on and off. That happens a lot with some.
Then they go dark.

COUPLE:
— you can't privatise freedom.
— They can sell anything they want.

GIRL:
To get back to –
I thought you would tell me –
What she –
I don't have much time –

COUPLE:
— that time
— the rebellion
— the selling
— the rebellion against the selling
— it was the time of the great floods. Mud and water
everwhere. The selling was like a flood. We watched the tide
rise. Sandbags. Couldn't stop it. It was on television. Water
lapping over the screens. Strange silence of desolation.
— Not the selling. That wasn't on television
— but we knew
— the way one knows and doesn't know. *(To the GIRL.)*
You know?
— the silence lapped around us
— but we knew. Like the floods. We didn't want to believe.
There are always warnings.
— Who knows…now that we remember what we didn't
know?

GIRL:
I came.

You said you had something. I thought it was – her. Maybe she
– wants to –

COUPLE:
— we've been saving this
— for you
— the beginning of your life
— your future
— you have future?

GIRL:
Future. Yes. Like career. Future career.

COUPLE:
— are they synonyms? Future, career?

GIRL:
I'm exceptional at numbers. I can teach maths at secondary school. I can go into a bank.

COUPLE:
— we suspected
— feared
— that's why we had to –

Very short beat.

— you can't go over to them
— sell yourself to them
— not after what we've done
— the rebellion
— and your mother
— that's why we lured
— attracted

GIRL:
I want to live in a city. You're not allowed unless you work for them. It's my life.

COUPLE:
— she gave it to you

GIRL:
There were texts, sometimes, a message, a voice. Then nothing. Nothing.

COUPLE:
— phones could be traced
— or cut off
— batteries died

GIRL:
If she's not – if you can't – there's nothing. I don't have time.

I apologize.

COUPLE:
— apologize?

GIRL:
What you do to stop a conversation. Apologize. I have it here.
Apologize and continue as before. Customers, constituents,
colleagues and co-sanguinists.

COUPLE:
— co-sanguinists?

GIRL:
Family. Without the emotion. Family is blinking on and off.

COUPLE:
— we didn't sell you
— we could have
— many times
— that was emotion
— love

GIRL:
Ok. Thank you.
But it's my life.

COUPLE:
— when you have our gift maybe –
— maybe you won't need to
— want to

GIRL:
I've made up my mind.
I don't need a gift.
That's not why I came. Basically. Yeah. That's not why I came.
I thought she –

I took the risk because I thought she –

COUPLE:
— we've kept it safe
— at great risk
— sacrifice

GIRL: *(Reading.)*
I really apologize. I sincerely apologize.
And I don't have sacrifice

COUPLE:
— we were living inside the town
— near the cathedral
— working
— you were at school. Primary school. Lovely school.

GIRL:
I don't remember. Did you record it?

COUPLE:
— we didn't record everything in those days
— we might have had a photograph
— but they were all confiscated when your mother joined
the rebels.

GIRL:
Left

COUPLE:
— it seemed right.

GIRL:
Right?

COUPLE:
— the right thing to do
— on the side of the suffering
— dispossessed
— unemployed
— disabled
— unthrusting.
— We encouraged her

GIRL:
You gave her the courage?
You let her leave?

COUPLE:
— we knew the risks

— but for the sake of
— the cheated
— homeless
— most, really
— refugees
— home refugees
— future refugees
— as opposed to the foreign serfs
— they weren't refugees then
— ordinary people they were called
— the ordinary
— for the future of the ordinary
— their homes were being sold
— their lives

GIRL:
They could buy them

COUPLE:
— with what?
— London was closed
— to the refugees
— that's the ordinary people.
— Then the southwest towns closed. Swindon. Basingstoke.
All sold.

GIRL:
Who wanted to live in Basingstoke?

COUPLE:
— the Russians who couldn't live in London
— Chinese
— British
— even the French
— you never knew.
— Then it started here
— the town was sold
— there were protests. Riots.
— We had our house but there was the street charge, the water
charge, the air charge, the school charge, the bedroom charge,
the window charge, the view charge, the pavement charge

— safety against terrorist attack charge. That broke us.
— And some said no
— she said no

GIRL:
She left

COUPLE:
— she had to
— the hills were still free
— over there.
— We took refuge here
— sanctuary
— it all happened very quickly
— exponentially

GIRL:
They had to sell. No one wanted to make anything. I went to
school. I know.

COUPLE:
— they didn't have to
— they chose to
— first the buildings
— then what was inside. The art. The skeletons. The maps.
The charters.
— They sold anything historical
— they sold history
— all the past
— they sold Shakespeare
— he used to be free
— to a Middle Eastern magnate
— no, to Putin
— all the books in all the libraries
— all they said because of the debt
— riot in the British Library
— she was involved in that
— sitting on books
— we think
— and all the contents here

— the last sanctuary. The last cathedral
— because it was the year of the celebration

GIRL:
Celebration?

COUPLE:
— commemoration
— 1215
— we were there.

GIRL:
You were there in 1215?

COUPLE:
— in a way.
— In those days you could remember
— the past became the present
— as you celebrated you brought the past back
— pageantry, theatre, paintings, talks, words, the meaning of –
the memory of – the origin of –

GIRL:
As in germ

COUPLE:
— the celebrations celebrated
— reminded
— that no one
— no thing
— no power had the right

GIRL:
Right? Again.
No.

COUPLE:
— to be absolute
— abusive
— inhuman
— it was in words
— the words of the rebellion

— against Kingship
— that was national Kingship
— before international Kingship
— the international monetary Kingship
— consolidated
— its absolute abusive and inhuman power
— but after the books and the papers and the maps and all the things and the buildings and the streets and the pavements and the gas and the oil and the air had all been sold, there wasn't much left.
— Only the words
— it was only a matter of time
— we didn't know
— but she knew, your mother.
— She came to warn us
— during the truce

GIRL:
Truce?

COUPLE:
— agreement that is inevitably broken

GIRL:
I know about broken agreements
I had a message: we agreed to meet
she never came

COUPLE:
— the truce was broken.
— All words were privatised. Traded. Sent abroad. Sometimes illegally smuggled. Hidden. Not allowed to use. She was involved in the break in – we think. That's when she was sold – we believe. We didn't hear. We waited
— she knew we were here
— that's why we stayed as long as
— because possibly one day
— hoping day after day
— but we never heard again.

77

GIRL:
So you don't know. If she – or how to find –
I came –

COUPLE:
— she would want you to have
— we're not saying continue
— but to know
— to consider
— and perhaps not agree
— with them

GIRL:
It's my life.
I don't want to end up –
And then what for?

COUPLE:
— we'd never bought shares in BP
— or in the Halifax
— or the Post Office
— or air
— but we bought a share
— of a word.
— it was that or a few ounces of gold.
— Like gold anyway.
— We have this share
— and that's your gift.
— Here's the certificate.
— Here's the word.
— It's yours. You own
— a share of it.

GIRL:
What is it?

COUPLE:
— it's from a quote

GIRL:
A quote?

COUPLE:
— a quote was something you knew by heart written by
someone else and you could say it

GIRL:
Without paying?

COUPLE:
— free
— I first heard it here in this cathedral
— they read it out as they were auctioning the real one
— the parchment
— we never knew who bought it
— it was taken away, never seen again, forgotten
— it might be in Switzerland. Many things are. Hong Kong.
Ulaanbaatar. With the copper. Or burnt
— but the dean had copied it
— it was one of her favourites
— June was with us here
— June married us
— June wrote it all down
— before she was sold
— we were quite a few then
— we're the last
— there isn't much time

GIRL:
If she's never –

COUPLE:
— listen.
— To no one shall we sell, to no one shall we deny or delay,
right or justice. That was the quote. And I bought the word as
it was auctioned – a share in: Justice.

GIRL:
I know about just
as in now. Very soon.

COUPLE:
— we know about that just too

— as in it was just what we expected
— we've just been told
— we just can't stay here
— we just can't be allowed
— that's just why we asked you
— to please just come. Now
— we'll just have to go
— just as the bell

GIRL: *(Checking her mobile.)*
But I don't have justice.

COUPLE:
— you have it now
— a share in
— it's our gift
— it's from her
— it's very valuable
— hold it
— guard it
— and when you use it
— handle with care
— don't ever sell

GIRL: *(On her app)*
Justice. It's not here. Look. Not even a flicker.
Are you sure it's valuable?
How can I be sure?
Or that it's from her? When I look for her
and hug only silence?
Are you sure it –

She turns out.

who can tell me what –
if–
it's even a word

Fade.

Sally Woodcock

PINK GIN

Characters

PRESIDENT	President of an East African country: black, fifties. Wears expensive dark suit and tie and a Lion King head dress.
ANGELICA/MAMA	P.A. / veteran freedom fighter: of uncertain age – but not young, black, female. Wears ragged animal skins, a huge rasta hat containing very long dreads. Over skins she wears incongruous office 'uniform' – jacket or dress. Around her neck is a large calabash (or gourd) on a long leather thong.
JASPER	Landowner / rancher: white, fifties. Scruffily dressed with ill-fitting blazer and club tie. He has a gun.
PLAYERS	Spirits of forest folk / freedom fighters through the ages: any age / gender / ethnicity. Unobtrusively dressed.
	Players should be numbered and have individual parts, depending on how many actors are available. Four would work well.

NOTES

The piece should be punctuated with diegetic sound by PLAYERS with hands / feet / voice to emphasise rain / the natural world.

The symbol (/) indicates overlapping dialogue.

The symbol (]) indicates speaking simultaneously.

Bold indicates raised voice.

SCENE 1

PRESIDENT's office in an African country. Present day.

Centre stage is a grandiose desk.

It is raining torrentially outside.

PRESIDENT paces the floor, muttering. He blocks his ears to blot out rain noise, but can't.

PLAYERS hang around in shadows. He does not see them.

PRESIDENT: 'Ladies and gentlemen.' *(Traces his finger down a list muttering.)* 'Gentlemen.' *(Pause.)* 'Karibuni! Bemvindos! Ahlan wa sahlan! Dopro pozalovat! Li ho! And welcome! To you all. Welcome and – and congratulations – on your interest in Africa Spectacular. In association with Walt Disney Resorts, the Shanghai Sh-shendi group, Oriental Lalalalaland Company, Foreste, Vnesheconombank. *(Beat.)* And the Muppets Studio.'

ANGELICA: *(Off – intercom.)* Your delegation is ready, Your Excellency.

He shakes the last few drops from a bottle of bitters into a crystal glass. He swills it around with intent. He pours in a large measure of gin and watches it turn pink, holding it up to the light. Succoured, he drinks.

PRESIDENT: 'Today is a great day in the future of this nation, this continent, the world. For no longer need international safari seekers look to the US, Paris, Tokyo, Shanghai or Hong Kong to meet with Simba the Lion, Rafiki the Baboon, Dumbo the elephant, Bambi the venison – or Pumbaa the fafafafaforest hog-roast hahahahahahaha: (A roar hear I think.) Rrrrrraaforrestaaaarrff…

ANGELICA: *(Off.)* Your Excellency, everyone is waiting.

He drinks.

PRESIDENT: No more need omnes visitors to Africa f-fear 'It's a Jungle Book out there,' hahahaha I'm a fun guy a funny guy queque!

He drinks.

ANGELICA: *(Off.)* The gentlemen are / all –

PRESIDENT: For today I offer you a window of opportunitit-tit-titty to invest in a venture the like of which this world has never seen. Today is your moment to secure a seat at a banquet of African delights which will be the envy of all mankind. Be it Ivory Towers, Hippotropolis or the Jumbo Jet-tit-tit-tit-ison …today is your chance to grab a golden ticket to an entertainment Kingdom which I hereby bequeath to posterity fosterity.

He looks up at 'rain', holds out hands to catch drops.

ANGELICA: *(Entering – behind PRESIDENT – he does not see her.)*

Shall I send them in, Your / Ex – ?

PRESIDENT: **NO-MNES.**: Angelica, This rain does not stop sunt sunt sunt sunt.

ANGELICA shrugs.

It has been raining for-for-for-for-for

ANGELICA:}   For ninety seven days.
PRESIDENT:}   For ninety seven days.

PRESIDENT: And the Angostura Bitters bottle: it is empty que que que que!

Bring more. *(She exits.)*

> *(Louder.)* 'Today, my friends with your most opportune support from the vvery fartland heartland of my nation's tatatatatata/t –

PLAYER: tropical and subtropical moist broadleaf / forest

PLAYER: tropical and subtropical dry broadleaf /forest

PLAYER: tropical and subtropical coniferous /forest

PLAYER: tropical broadleaf and mixed /forests

PLAYER: boreal coniferous /forests

PLAYER: tropical and sub-tropical /grasslands

PLAYER: savannas

PLAYER: highlands

PLAYER: wetlands

PLAYER: – and Afrotropic xeric shrubland –

Pause.

PRESIDENT: – will rise nine hundred and ninety nine thousand acres of fully air-conditioned undercover duplex multiplex safari-style splendour deafforestentur –

Stops. Pours gin in glass but fails to shake any more bitters. Drinks it down in one. Grimaces.

> omnes foreste que afforestate sunt tempore nostro: – Omnes foreste que – Omnes foreste que –
>
> **Angelica!**

ANGELICA: Your Excellency?

PRESIDENT: **Bring more bitters forestate.**

ANGELICA: Unfortunately we are having difficulty acquiring Angostura bitters at present, Your Excellency: the supplier in Trinidad is having something of a … liquidity crisis.

PRESIDENT: **Bring more** que afforestate sunt.

ANGELICA: We are doing our level best, I assure you. Meanwhile, the gentlemen are on very tight schedules –

PRESIDENT: Angelica, I cannot statim spatim statim /sp –

ANGELICA: Speak? *(Beat.)* But, Your Excellency: speak you must! This is your Big Day: today you stand on the cusp of greatness: –

PRESIDENT: Omnes foreste que afforestate there it goes again omnes omnes –

ANGELICA: Your Excellency, / I really –

PRESIDENT: What is this Angelica statim statim?

Pause.

ANGELICA: I am familiar with many local dialects, Your Excellency, but this is not one I / recognise –

PRESIDENT: It's not a dialect, woman: it's Latin! Tempore.

ANGELICA: Latin tempore?

PRESIDENT: Angelicle why is Latin slop-slop slopping about in mum mum mum my mouth mostro nostro?

ANGELICA: Slopping about in / your – ?

PRESIDENT: Slipping in slopping out momnes omnes nomnes! Every time I mention statim statim – there it goes again – what is happening to me Angelica?

ANGELICA:	*(Standing very close behind him.)* Every time you mention what? Exactly? Your Excellency?
PRESIDENT:	La-la-la-la –
ANGELICA:	Land?
PRESIDENT:	Aff-aff-aff-aff –
ANGELICA:	And forest? Every time you mention land – or forest – Latin slips in and slops out of your mouth.
PRESIDENT:	This is not normal. Is it?
ANGELICA:	Your Excellency, who am I to say what is normal?

Pause.

	Though what I must say is that the gentlemen have travelled from / all corners of the globe –
PRESIDENT:	Que afforestate que afforestate –
ANGELICA:	– and are most anxious to place their bids:
PRESIDENT:	sunt tempore nostro –
ANGELICA:	I really must press you, Your Excellency –
PRESIDENT:	Statim statim statim sunt –
ANGELICA:	The gentleman from Shang Hai has a helicopter waiting, Mr Shullakshullah has urgent business at the camel abatoir the Duke of Djibouti / is –
PRESIDENT:	**Send them away que que que!**
ANGELICA:	Very well … I shall tell them at present his Excellency is indisposed since he has Latin slipping in and slopping out –

PRESDIENT:	**Ixnay!**
ANGELICA:	Well they will need some plausible explanation.
PRESIDENT:	*(Trying to shake a drop of bitters into his glass.)* Tell them I find myself not feeling very … rosy nosy nostro.
ANGELICA:	'His Excellency is not feeling very rosy nosy / nos –'?
PRESIDENT:	Tell them I am not in the pink.
ANGELICA:	'Not in the / pink'?
PRESIDENT:	Omnes bittores **more bitters**.
ANGELICA:	Your Excellency, as I said, there really are none to be –
PRESIDENT:	**I NEED PINK GIN! Raarrrrrrrrrffffffff!**

Pause.

ANGELICA:	I will see what I can do.

SCENE 2

PRESIDENT at desk, head in hands, ANGELICA, now barefoot, behind. It is still raining torrentially.

ANGELICA:	We have grounded all outbound flights, flown in a troop of topless Tokani and some vintage Bogandan champagne.

Pause.

PRESIDENT:	What about the guy from Shanghai?
ANGELICA:	Comatose. The Bogandan champagne is a great success.
PRESIDENT:	He's b-bidding for for for / for

ANGELICA: – for the conservation station, trunk towers, poachers' alley, jungle jalopies, coconut casino and the cheetah express.

(He nods, dumbly.) He is going nowhere.

(Patting him, maternally.) Now.
Your Excellency. What would you like first?
The good news, the mixed news – *(Beat.)* –
or the bad news.

PRESIDENT: Que!

PRESIDENT puts his hand up to his shoulder, almost sobbing. ANGELICA holds it, tenderly.

ANGELICA: Let's start with the good news, shall we?

PRESIDENT nods dumbly.

Our research has been fruitful.

(Producing a document.) We have identified the slippy sloppy Latin which is tangulating your tongue. *(Beat.)* It is Clause 47 of England's Magna Carta. *(Reading.)* Magna Carta, a.k.a. the 'great charter' was presented to England's King John in 1215 by a posse of medieval barons / who –

PRESIDENT: **I know what Magna Carta is!** It is the cornerstone of our own great constitution! Crafted by my grandfather's own fair hand! Let me remind you I studied the Law at Oxford, Cambridge, Aberystwyth and Kampala universities so I know all about Magna Carta thank you very much. I regret my Latin is a little rusty but I know enough to deduce an ap-proximate translation: that is to say – that is to say – that is to say –

PLAYER: All forest

PLAYER: which has been afforested

PLAYER: in our time

PLAYER: shall be disafforested.

PRESIDENT: That is to say

PLAYER: All forest

PLAYER: which has been afforested

PLAYER: in our time

PLAYER: shall be disafforested.

PRESIDENT: What the fa-fa-fa-fa-/fa-?

ANGELICA: Now let me see *(Reading.)*:

'All forests' – for 'forests' read: 'not only woodland but wetland, pasture, bog, ditch, pit, marl or any other god-given communal resource';

'which have been afforested' – for 'afforested' read 'appropriated', 'gazetted', 'privatised' or stolen;

'in our time' – for 'our time' read 'as far back as we or any of our forbears can remember';

'must be disafforested' – for 'disafforested' read 'given back'.

PRESIDENT: Given back?

ANGELICA: Which all seems pretty normal.

PRESIDENT: **Normal?** To find myself tongue tangulated by omnes osbsolete clause from a document signed eight hundred years ago on a small damp European island six thousand kilometres away? Me, fourth self-appointed democratic leader of an East African republic

in the 21st century? I do nomnes consider this
to be na-normal!

ANGELICA: No. No you're quite right: that part is anti-na-
normal.

PRESIDENT: Anti-na-normal?

ANGELICA: Post-na-normal.

PRESIDENT: Post-na-normal?

ANGELICA: And para-na-normal.

PRESIDENT: Pa? Pa? Pa? / Pa?

ANGELICA: Which brings me to the mixed news.

PRESIDENT: Afforestate!

ANGELICA: Indeed.

It would very much appear the question of
forest has become a particular stumbling
block –

PRESIDENT: Deafforestentur!

ANGELICA: Quite so! I have, therefore, taken it upon
myself to consult with a council of forest
elders from the Nyandaharushiruarua –

PRESIDENT: The Nya – ? *(Beat.)* That is my ancestral
home.

ANGELICA: Indeed. It is also mine. And it is also,
of course, the locus of your proposed
development – which you are – of course
fully entitled to develop however you so
choose. *(Beat.)* Since you have some pieces
of paper.

PRESIDENT: I possess nine hundred and ninety thousand
acres of / t-t-t-t-t- *(Beat.)* – title deeds

PLAYERS:	*(Mimicking.)* T-t-t-t-t-t- *(Beat.)* – title deeds

PRESIDENT:	Bestowed upon my grand-f-father / in 1963
ANGELICA:}	In 1963
PLAYERS:}	In 1963

PRESIDENT:}	At Lancaster House
ANGELICA:}	At Lancaster House
PLAYERS:}	At Lancaster House

PRESIDENT:}	In the new administration.
ANGELICA:}	In the new administration.
PLAYERS:}	In the new administration.

Beat.

ANGELICA:	We are all well aware.

PRESIDENT:	Statim que que que what did the elders say?

ANGELICA:	Your Excellency, I must warn you: once in possession – of these – the elders – findings – I fear there can be no turning back. Are you certain you wish to … find?

PRESIDENT:	Circus.

ANGELICA:	Very well. We – they – that is to say the elders – believe your plan has invoked the wrath of a particular … woman.

PRESIDENT:	Wo-wo-/woh-!

ANGELICA:	An old woman.

PRESIDENT:	O-o-/oh-!

ANGELICA:	A very old woman.

PRESIDENT:	Veh-veh-/veh-!

ANGELICA:	A very old – very angry – woman. From the Nyandaharushiruarua.

PRESIDENT:	What does she want sunt?

ANGELICA: She wants to live by the forest.

PRESIDENT: By the fo-fo-fo-fo-/fo -

ANGELICA: As she and her forbears have done or endeavoured to do for some several centuries. 'In tempore nostro'.

PRESIDENT: Do I nostro-nostro know her?

ANGELICA: Yes. And no.

PRESIDENT: Quiz?

ANGELICA: Well she is always there.

PRESIDENT: Quere? *(Rhymes with 'hair'.)*

ANGELICA: Oh – here and there – and – well – everywhere. These days.

Since now there is nowhere.

PRESIDENT: I nostro no such woman.

ANGELICA: No. That is rather the point. *(Beat.)* Which has proved a source of – frustration – to her. Over the past nine decades. *(calabash)* – and which may, at this critical time, have led her into a little … shall we say … monkey business.

PRESIDENT: Mum mum mum?

ANGELICA: Your Excellency, the elders believe this woman has taken to tangulating your tongue with the pink prose of the peasant –

PRESIDENT: – tap tip pip –

ANGELICA: though how she is achieving such a feat is quite beyond us

PRESIDENT: Fi-fi-fo-

ANGELICA: – let alone how a forest-dwelling woman of the Nyandaharushiruarua has accessed this 'obsolete' clause with which to so-tangulate.

PRESIDENT: Tap tap tip nip **NIPPLE**!

Pause.

ANGELICA: Well: it's very funny you should say that, Your Excellency. Because – we – they – that is to say – the elders – believe there may indeed be a lactatious element to this titular tale:

PRESIDENT: Tit tit tit/tit?

ANGELICA: she is, after all, known as Mama Ngoma.

Pause.

PRESIDENT: **Mumumum/um?**

ANGELICA: So you do know her!

PRESIDENT: **Mumumum/um!**

ANGELICA: Mother of the Forest! And celebrated freedom fighter!

PRESIDENT: **Mumumum/um!**

ANGELICA: Mama Ngoma! Who gave her youth, risked her life, made weapons, passed secrets, slew wild beasts, fought harder than any man, held out in the wilderness longer than any comrade including your own grandfather –

PRESIDENT: **Bob bob bot –**

ANGELICA: And was raped with a bottle for her efforts: the very same! And there were we – they – the elders – thinking you'd never heard of her! That you'd forgotten all about her!

PRESIDENT: **Ha-ha-ha-ha-ha-**

ANGELICA: Her hair? My goodness, you know about that too: that's right! Mama Ngoma has not cut her hair since 1952 –

PRESIDENT: **Ny-ny-ny-fif-fif-fif-!**

ANGELICA: – the year our comrades took up arms! Exactly! And she will not cut it until the freedom she fought for is won! Or her lands returned which, as everyone knows, amounts to the same thing. Clearly she feels that day has not yet / come.

PRESIDENT: **Lol-lol-lol-/lol –**

ANGELICA: Long? *(Beat.)* Her hair? *(Beat.)* Oh yes. As you'd expect. After all this time. *(Beat.)* Her hair is her history.

PLAYER: Her hair –

PLAYER:} is her history
PLAYER:} is her history

PLAYERS: *(All.)* Her hair is her history.

PLAYER: So long –

ANGELICA: – so they say –

PLAYER: – you know not –

ANGELICA: – so they say –

PLAYER: – where the woman / ends

PLAYER: – and the roots / begin –

PLAYER: – with the snow-topped / mountain –

PLAYER: – at the roots of the / crown –

PLAYER: – with the roots of the / trees –

PLAYER: – on the black forest / floor.

ANGELICA: So they say.

ANGELICA passes her calabash to a player. She produces full bottle of bitters and 'pinks' his gin: Meanwhile the PLAYERS pass the calabash around as his head spins to the sound. He drinks, dazed and confused, but too relieved to question or think straight.

ANGELICA: So you do know Mama Ngoma!
     (Takes back calabash.)

PRESIDENT: Qua-qha-qua-?

ANGELICA: I beg your pardon, Your Excellency?

PRESIDENT: Wha-wha-wha-?

PLAYER: *(Mocking.)* Qha-qha-qha?

PLAYER: Wha-wha-wha?

PRESIDENT: Qua-qua-qua-wha-wha-wha-?

PLAYERS: Qua-qua-qua-wha-wha-wha-?

ANGELICA: Wha-wha-what is … *(Disbelieving.)* Ngoma?

PLAYERS: *(All.)* **WHAT IS … NGOMA?**

The rain gets heavier.

ANGELICA: But, Your Excellency, surely – ? You do not
     – ? And yet you are – ? Are you not African?
     Are you not African of Africans!

PRESIDENT opens and shuts his mouth like a fish.

PLAYERS laugh and mock. They move around him. He hears / 'feels' them but does not see them.

ANGELICA, in the background, still unseen to him, almost imperceptibly 'conducts' the players. PRESIDENT, chicken-like, takes on a rhythmic dance as PLAYERS generate a background beat / hum with voice / hands / feet.

PLAYER: Ngoma is drum

PLAYER: Ngoma is dance

PLAYER: Ngoma beat

PLAYER: Ngoma is trance;

The chant speeds up, punctuated by calabash.

PLAYER: Ephemeral

PLAYER: mercurial

PLAYER: mutable

PLAYER: protean

PLAYER: capricious

PLAYER: ethereal

PLAYER: terrestrial

PLAYER: celestial

PLAYER: visceral

PLAYER: voluble

PLAYER: soluble

PLAYER: malleable

PLAYER: animal

PLAYER: vegetal

PLAYER: mineral

PLAYER: skeletal;

PLAYER: ingrown

PLAYER: unknown

PLAYER: Unseeable

PLAYER: Unknowable;

His head jerks back and forth, his legs twitch until he is screeching in extreme distress.

PRESIDENT: **Angelica! Angelica! Angelicacacacacacaca!**

She goes to him.

ANGELICA: Hush hush hush hush hush whatever is the matter? Hush...

She tenderly covers his eyes, he clings to her.

PRESIDENT: What the fah-fah-fah is happening to me?

ANGELICA: It is raining, that is all: hush hush.

PRESIDENT: Make it stop **Angelica**!

ANGELICA: *(She covers his ears.)* Your Excellency, I cannot stop the rain. Who do you think I am? *(She stops the rain. PLAYERS melt off. He relaxes.)*

ANGELICA: And now for the bad news. *(Beat.)* Despite all our best efforts I'm afraid we are simply unable to locate any Angostura Bitters. We've exhausted every known supplier across Britain and every former colony, including the United States of America. Our search goes on of course. But so far in vain. Which is, of course, most unfortunate. Knowing how much you have come to enjoy this particular tinge to your tipple.

PRESIDENT: **Nipple.**

ANGELICA: Indeed.

Your Excellency, I – we – they – can think of only one solution.

PRESIDENT: Nip-nip-nip?

ANGELICA: You send for an Englishman.

PRESIDENT: N-n-n-n-nomnes **NOT – NO!** *(Silence. He puffs up.)* I do **not** and will **not** fraternise with the English ever again! Fraternising with the English is a backward retrogressive 20th Century pursuit. My grandfather may have had his reasons for shaking hands with those in-bred bastard British barons who herded my kinsmen into reserves like donkeys and dik diks! But why should I? And why would I? When I have brand new friends from China, Russia, the United Arab Emirates, Brazil, Belarus and the Islands of Scilly? All falling over each other for a teeny tiny titty tit bit of a new ancient ergonomic Africa conceived and – and – consecrated by me! *(Beat.)* Why ever would I do that?

ANGELICA: Good question, Your Excellency. Very good question.

And very eloquently put. If I may say so. Splendidly put. *(Aside.)* If a little confused. *(To him.)* The rhetoric of a true freedom fighter. *(Aside.)* I think. *(Beat.)* Well done.

PRESIDENT: Omnes – omnes – / om-om-om-

ANGELICA: However, it is our – their – the elders' belief that a secret source of this missing – ingredient – may yet lurk in a region of the Nyandaharushiruarua hidden from all human – or should I say – African – eyes –

PRESIDENT: *(Excited.)* Statim statim statim / statim –

ANGELICA: Coincidentally the only region not yet engulfed by – that is to say – earmarked – by – your magnificent – development – at least not entirely; namely: the area under preservation – I beg your pardon – 'conservation' – by the wazungu.

PRESIDENT: The wazungu!

ANGELICA: Who, though 'African' in name, are,
as is plain to see, spawn of the pink-
faced invader hell-bent on keeping the
Nyandaharushiruarua exactly the way it
was before Africa contained any two-legged
Africans at all!

PRESIDENT: **Defelephant!**

ANGELICA: Precisely. *(Beat.)*

And this is the problem we have.

Pause. PRESIDENT is sweating. ANGELICA pours him another gin. He attempts in vain to 'pink' it.

PRESIDENT: Ginman ginman ginman ginman ...

ANGELICA: I beg your pardon, Your Excellency...

PRESIDENT: Ginman ginman ginman ginman ...

ANGELICA: How extraordinary! *(He gobbles like a turkey.)*
Goodness me: we've been thinking along
the same lines all along! *(Beat.)* Well let's not
delay a minute longer. Let's give your old
friend Jasper Ginman a call.

PRESIDENT: **NIX**.

ANGELICA: Nix?

PRESIDENT: Jasper Ginman is not my forestate friend!

ANGELICA: Perhaps not. But your respective families
have been neighbours since 1963. He
also has some pieces of paper. And it was,
let's not forget, Jasper's own grandfather
James 'Jimmy' Giman who first gave your
grandfather the secret recipe for your
beloved pink tipple – I have been fielding Mr
Ginman's persistent calls most ferociously of

late, but, under the circumstances – do you not think it may – well – be time for a little – neighbourly – chat?

PRESIDENT: Quamobrem?

ANGELICA: Well, let's see now shall we: *(Tracing map.)* Currently it seems Flamingo Flyover will cross Ginman's dam at one end. Pelican Crossings passes through his forest in one two three – four places... The Angolan Barbecue is now – where are we now? In his kitchen; Wildebeest Stampede engulfs about two thirds of his ... er: verandah. And Wrecking Ball Alley crashes through his bedroom. Nothing untoward. In the scheme of things. But he has been grumbling a little. *(Beat.)* It may be time to remind him who is ... boss? *(He gobbles.)* Which, as well as solving your refreshment needs would demonstrate once and for all just exactly where your loyalties lie... Which would surely appease our mischievious ... Mama Ngoma? *(He gobbles.)* We could have him here by lunch time...? Just in time for a small- pink-cocktail? *(He nods dumbly.)*

Meantime, why don't you have a little browse through this.

(She produces charter of the forest and lays it before him.) The Second Charter. Poor relation, if you like, to the legendary Magna Carta – with which you are so familiar. Also known as The Charter of the Forest. A later elaboration, if you like, of the humble clause 47. You will know it of course. But, with Mr Ginman on the way, it may just refresh your ... *(She produces some bitters and shakes some drops into his gin.)* ... long-term memory. As to how things ... currently stand. Land-wise. If you like.

PRESIDENT: *(Amazed at the appearance of bitters.)* How – ?

ANGELICA: Oh just a little knack. *(Exits. He drinks. Opens book.)*

PRESIDENT: *(Muttering.)* Clause 47? Second Charter? All forests ... which have been afforested... in our time ...

SCENE 3

PRESIDENT's office. Drinks tray is thoroughly replenished. JASPER stands, awkwardly. PRESIDENT, giddy with anticipation, swills bitters around a glass, fills it with gin and watches it turn pink.

PRESIDENT: There she blows hahaha: and Plymouth Gin, no less! Navy strength in tempore: very nice. Always said the London stuff's too dry to do justice to nostro pink stuff – filthy brew if you ask me hahahaha – but this is just the ticket just the tickety ticket ...

He downs his drink and smacks his lips, laughing in near-hysterical relief. JASPER has no drink or seat.

JASPER: We aim to please, Your Excellency hahahaha.

PRESIDENT: *(Sated.)* By god that's good. *(He shudders, sits luxuriously, pours another. JASPER eyes a chair but does not sit.)*

               Now Jasper hahaha *(Seeping with relief.)*: omnes foreste que afforestate sunt tempore nostro statim deafforestentur. *(Beat.)* Words which will ring loud and clear for you of all people.

               Hm? *(Pause.)*

JASPER: I'm sorry?

PRESIDENT: I should damn well think you are! 1066 and all that – well – 1215 for sake of argument: 'in tempore nostro' ... you know what I mean.

104

JASPER: Do I?

PRESIDENT: You always were a contrary bloody lot, you English. You certainly know my Achilles Heel I'll give you that haha. I'm assuming there's omnes foreste where this came from? *(Mixes another gin.)*

JASPER: As long as you have us you have your supply, Your Excellency.

PRESIDENT: Yes haha. *(Settling again.)* Now. Remind me, Jasper, who are my other neighbours these days? Up on the Nyandahahaha/ha-?

JASPER: *(Nervous.)* Well – uh – me, as ever, on two sides though you are still the majority landowner 'by a country mile' as they say hahaha.

PRESIDENT: Haha yes you do sunt. *(Drinking.)* And down the hill to the West?

JASPER: Uh – well that'll be the – uh – that'll be the Whiteheads –

PRESIDENT: Across the v-valley?

JASPER: The Wingham-Whytes –

PRESIDENT: And on the far side of the afforestate?

JASPER: Andy Redman. And sons.

PRESIDENT: How many statim?

JASPER: Five: Mathew, Mark, Luke, John and Llewellyn.

PRESIDENT: And to the nostro north?

JASPER: Peter English.

PRESIDENT: So omnes neighbours are English?

JASPER: No no no no. Andy Redman is Welsh. *(Beat.)* By descent, at least: though we are all of course African born and bred – very much so: 'more African than the Africans' you might / say

PRESIDENT: Well deafforestentur you'll all have to go.

Pause.

JASPER: Go?

PRESIDENT: Go.

JASPER: Go ... where?

PRESIDENT: Back to England of course. Or Wales. From whence you came! Though I'll have the contents of your drinks cabinets foreste: Angelica! *(Enters.)* Impound the necessary prior to deportment.

ANGELICA: Consider it done, Your Excellency. *(She exits with the bitters – giving JASPER the finger as she goes, he does not see.)*

JASPER: Deportment? N-n-n-b-b-but – but – ?

PRESIDENT: You've over-stepped the mark, Jasper. Pestering my personal assistant with your trivial pursuits –

JASPER: Trivial? / Hardly –

PRESIDENT: I am a tolerant man: I may have turned a blind eye to your continued existence on the foreste fringes of my new develephant **development** *(Beat.)* providing you'd had the decency to tolerate a little encroachment here and there –

JASPER: A little encroachment!

PRESIDENT: We might have come to some arrangement
             – one can never have too many flamingo or
             pygmy hippopotami –

JASPER: **NO FUCKING WAY!** *(Beat.)* Your Excellency.

PRESIDENT: I beg your tempore!

JASPER: You can't just throw me – us – out! Not now!
             Not anymore. NO!

PRESIDENT: Why can't I?

JASPER: Because – because it's bloody beautiful up
             there! Our side of the Nyandaharushiruarua,
             Tom's, Andy's, George's and mine, is one
             of the last pristine wildernesses in Africa –
             and we – we – between us – we host five
             hundred and forty-six species of indigenous
             wildlife including some of our planet's most
             noble and endangered land mammals, all
             precariously – and expensively – protected
             within an extremely fragile fast-diminishing
             ecological treasure trove of – of – of –
             tropical and subtropical moist broadleaf
             forest, tropical and subtropical dry broadleaf
             forest, tropical and subtropical coniferous
             forest, tropical broadleaf and mixed forests,
             boreal coniferous forests, tropical and sub-
             tropical grasslands, savannah, highland,
             wetland and Afrotropic xeric shrubland.

Calabash. Pause.

             And because we, our fathers, and our fathers'
             fathers have strived ruthlessly and and and –
             ruthlessly – to keep it that way for / for –

PRESIDENT: For whom?

JASPER: For Prince William! *(Pause.)*

PRESIDENT: For Prince William?

JASPER: Yes! … Yes. But not not just Prince William
– there's there's others –

PRESIDENT: Which others?

JASPER: Prince Harry. And – and – Kate – and the
sister – Pippy Plumbottom, just took up safari
marathons (my word you should see her
go); And there's – there's – Joanna Lumley,
there's Richard Branson, there's Ronnie
Wood, Rory Bremner, Griff Rhys Jones,
Ruby Wax, Ben Fogle, Alistair McGowan,
Elton John, Zoe Ball; to name a few – and
– between you and me Will himself's most
likely stopping by next week: I've some new
quad bikes. *(Beat.)* Do join us / if you –

PRESIDENT: It is time to go.

JASPER: With respect … I don't think you mean that,
Your Excellency.

Think of your reputation on the international
stage.

You, Sir, are a Renaissance man. A great
modern leader.

For more than a century your nation has
been the destination of choice for presidents
and princes; Hollywood stars, eminent
conservationists; all seeking sanctuary
in a land of unparalleled adventure,
unfathomable splendour, beauty beyond
compare.

And there you stand – centre stage – our
visionary leader.

With the wisdom to harness this land's
bounteous gifts – old and new – to the
greater good of all mankind.

In defending our continuing efforts – up in
the Nyandaharushiruarua – you are the man
who, at a time of unprecedented change,
of inevitable progress, nationally, globally,
universally, has the foresight to preserve our
natural heritage.

A gift from God – on high –

You please your country; the world; you
please God –

PRESIDENT: **But I do not please Mama Ngoma.**

JASPER: Mama – who? *(Pause.) (ANGELICA enters,
JASPER senses but does not see her.)* **Ahaaaaah!**
So that's what all this is about. *(He holds out a
glass. She pours his gin.)* Bloody nuisance that
woman. *(He takes it.)* Ignore her.

PRESIDENT: Ignore her?

JASPER: Absolutely. *(She pulls up a chair for him.
He sits.)* Ignore her and she'll go away,
old boy. *(Drinks.)* Only way.

(ANGELICA retreats into shadow.)

PRESIDENT: But – but – but – You … know her?

JASPER: Well I wouldn't say I know her. Per se.
Though I certainly know of her: don't we all?
Bloody woman: we've evicted her from our
forests umpteen times she turns back up like
a bad smell, rattling her bloody rattle, leaving
her detritus under the mugumo tree …

PRESIDENT: *(In awe.)* You've seen Mama Ngoma under
the mugumo tree?

JASPER: No: don't get to see her. She has this hair you
know.

Which rather … gets in the way. Forest wise.

PRESIDENT: The hair! *(Beat.)* How do you know of the ha-ha-ha-ha-/ha-?

JASPER: Oh, you know: hearsay…

PLAYER: white at the / roots

PLAYER: white at the / roots

PLAYER: as the mountain /top

PLAYER: as the mountain /top

PLAYER: black /at the roots

PLAYER: black at the / roots

PLAYER: of the forest / floor –

PLAYER: of the forest floor –

JASPER: Hasn't had a haircut for sixty years. *(Beat.)* So they say.

PRESIDENT: Who? Says?

JASPER: Oh no one you'd notice. But you can hear her rattling on …

PLAYER shakes the calabash quietly.

PLAYERS: *(All – quietly.)* Mzungu aende ulaya, Mwafrika apata uhuru.

JASPER: On and on …

PLAYERS: *(Repeating.)* Mzungu aende ulaya, Mwafrika apata uhuru.

JASPER: *(Over.)* ulaya uhuru – this thing you know – apata ulaya – gets in your head– mzungu aende – bloody nuisance – as I say … ulaya ulaya Trick is: shut it out, man – uhuru uhuru – don't let it get to you – apata aende – nothing but a figment!

PRESIDENT: A figment?

JASPER: Superstitious load of old clap trap! / Mzungu
aende ulaya –

PLAYERS: *(Louder.)* Mzungu aende ulaya, Mwafrika
apata uhuru.

*PLAYERS pass calabash; one PLAYER fills two glasses and hands
them to the men. They both drink deeply.*

JASPER: *(Louder.)* Got to get a grip! Apata uhuru…

PRESIDENT: Get a grip …

JASPER: Remember: you're a modern man!
Aende ulaya …

PRESIDENT: – *(Drinking.)* modern man –

JASPER: *(Moving with PLAYERS.)* Show her who's boss.
Mwafrika apata…

PRESIDENT: – *(Drinking.)* Show her who's boss –

JASPER: **Stick to your guns, Your Excellency!**
(Grabs his gun.) OY! Out my way, you!
(Pushes PLAYER aside.)

PLAYERS:}   *(Louder.)* Mzungu aende ulaya, Mwafrika apata
uhuru.

JASPER:}   Mzungu … ulaya … uhuru.

JASPER: *(To PLAYERS.)* Shoo! Shoo! Can't see the
woods … trees trees – Where is she? Guns
trees guns trees: know she's here somewhere
mzungu mzungu I'll get her aende
(To PRESIDENT.) Rise above it, old boy! Mind
over matter! *(To PLAYER.)* Oy! You! Get off
my land!

PRESIDENT: Mind over matter? *(Following calabash,
blindly.)*

JASPER: *(Following calabash.)* Aende… You'll see who's boss alaya alaya, you'll see who's forest uhuru: – trees forest – oy – oy – gun gun gun – **only thing for it, Your Excellency**:
I'LL SHOOT HER!

He grabs gun and takes aim.

PRESIDENT: *(Booming.)* **IXNAY!**

PLAYERS freeze.

You will not shoot her.

JASPER: Really? Seems a shame. She is a poacher after all.

PRESIDENT: **She is not a poacher**. She is a fugitive freedom fighter.

JASPER: Same thing really. With respect. *(Beat.)* Isn't it?

PRESIDENT: *(Thinks.)* Is it?

JASPER, now fully 'in the forest' brandishes his gun. PLAYERS tease him with the faint sound of calabash.

JASPER: Hear that? There she is now! I'll get her Woods … trees: Hear that?

PLAYERS: *(Barely audible.)* Mzungu aende ulaya, Mwafrika apata uhuru.

PRESIDENT: *(Listening intently.)* Hear … what?

PLAYERS:} Mzungu aende ulaya, Mwafrika apata uhuru
JASPER:} Mzungu aende ulaya, Mwafrika apata uhuru

The chant builds. JASPER is now in the thick of it, losing himself in the chant in spite of himself.

PRESIDENT: *(Stock still.)* Who speaks this vile thing? Are you who I think you are? This oath is forbidden! **You will not say it!**

PLAYERS   *(All.)* Omnes foreste
                 que afforeste
                 sunt tempore nostro
                 statim deafforestentur
                 (Building.)
                 Omnes foreste
                 que afforestate
                 sunt tempore nostro
                 statim deafforestentur

Continue as necessary until …

MAMA is revealed: in animal skins with matted hair all around.
PLAYERS place / examine her hair in wonderment. JASPER and
PRESIDENT are agog.

PRESIDENT: Shoot! **Shoot I say! Ginman I command**
                 you to SHOOT!

JASPER shoots. Rain stops. PLAYERS peel away.

Only MAMA remains, facing the men. Silence.

PRESIDENT: Mama … ?

JASPER: Ngoma … ?

She falls. Calabash rolls to a stop. They watch.

JASPER: There you go! Well-placed bullet usually does
                 the trick.

PRESIDENT: *(Tentative.)* Gentlemen. *(Steps over MAMA.)*
                 Karibuni. Bem-vindos. Ablan wa sahlan
                 dopro pozalovat li ho welcome and thank
                 you for your interest in Africa Spectacular
                 in association with Walt Disney Resorts
                 Shanghai Shendi group Oriental Land
                 Company Vnesheconombank *(Beat.)*
                 and the Muppets Studio: I am cured!

JASPER: *(Slapping him on the back.)* What did I tell you?
                 Mind over matter, old boy!

PRESIDENT: Call the delegation! Mama Ngoma is dead!
The Nyandaharusharururua is free! *(Looks up.)* The rain has stopped! *(Euphoric.)* Africa Spectacular will rise at last!

JASPER: Ah yuh, about that, Africa – um – thing –
I wondered if we could have a little word …

PRESIDENT: Angelica? I am ready! Angelica! Send them in!

SCENE 4

PRESIDENT's office. MAMA's body same place, hair all around. PRESIDENT downstage in lion head dress. PLAYERS generate faint applause/chatter in foreign tongues. PRESIDENT removes headdress, steps over MAMA, goes to desk.

PRESIDENT: I was magnificent, Angelica, was I not?
It was a triumph. I **am triumphant**!
I AM A TRIUMPH!

Sits luxuriously. Picks up bottles. All are empty.

Angelica! *(Looks all around.)* **Angelica!**
(Listens.)

(Searches for bottles, finds none. Exits.) Angelica!
More Gin! Angelica! More Tipple! Angelica!
Ginny gin gin! Tipple tipple! Angelica!
Tipple tipple! Nipply nipple!

He enters, frantic, ransacking bottles again, spinning in circles, shaking, disorientated, becoming child-like, infantile.

Angelica? Angelica! T-t-t-tipple! Pinky
pink! T-t-tipple! Pinkypinkle! Angeliccle
Angeliccle! tickle tickle! **Angeliccle!**

He trips over her body.

Angeliccle! Ah thank heaven ah
Angelicum ah ah ah ah … Angellimum
Angellymamamamam-m-m-m-mmmmm….

He lies beside her, rolls her to face him, nestles in, embryonically, entwining himself in her hair, and feeds from her, lustily.

PLAYER: All the forests which king Henry our
            grandfather made forest to the injury of him
            whose wood it was, it shall be disafforested.

            All woods made forest by king Richard our
            uncle or by King John our father shall be
            immediately disafforested.

            Every free man shall henceforth without
            being prosecuted agist his wood in the forest
            as he wishes and have his pannage, estover
            and turbary on condition that it does not
            harm any neighbour.

            No one shall henceforth lose life or limb
            because of our venison.

            These customs and liberties we have granted
            to everybody in forests and outside to be
            observed in our kingdom as far as pertains to
            clerks as well as laymen and by all men.

PRESIDENT collapses, sated. MAMA joins players.

PLAYERS:}   And if I fail to do this
ANGELICA   May this oath kill me
/MAMA:}   May this seven kill me
                May this meat kill me
                And if I fail to do this
                May this oath kill me
                May this seven kill me
                May this drink kill me.

ANGELICA   And if you fail to do this
/MAMA:}   May this oath kill you
                May this seven kill you
                May this meat kill you
                May this drink kill you.

End.

www.ingramcontent.com/pod-product-compliance
Ingram Content Group UK Ltd.
Pitfield, Milton Keynes, MK11 3LW, UK
UKHW031250020325
455689UK00008B/130